Time Tactics of
Very Successful People

Time Tactics of
Very Successful People

B. EUGENE GRIESSMAN, PH.D.

McGRAW-HILL, INC.
New York   San Francisco   Washington, D.C.   Auckland   Bogotá
Caracas   Lisbon   London   Madrid   Mexico City   Milan
Montreal   New Delhi   San Juan   Singapore
Sydney   Tokyo   Toronto

Library of Congress Cataloging-in-Publication Data

Griessman, B. Eugene.
 Time tactics of very successful people / B. Eugene Griessman.
   p.   cm.
 Includes bibliographical references and index.
 ISBN 0-07-024644-0
 1. Time management.   I. Title.
HD69.T54G75   1994
658.4'093—dc20   94-7532
                                                              CIP

McGraw-Hill

A Division of The **McGraw·Hill** Companies

16 17 18 19 DOC/DOC 0 9 8 7 6 5 4 3 2 1

ISBN 0-07-024644-0

*The sponsoring editor for this book was Betsy Brown, the editing
supervisor was Jane Palmieri, and the production supervisor was
Suzanne Babeuf. It was set in Palatino by McGraw-Hill's
Professional Book Group composition unit.*

Printed and bound by R. R. Donnelley & Sons Company.

This book is printed on recycled, acid-free paper
containing a minimum of 50% recycled, de-inked
fiber.

Contents

Preface

I once asked Stanley Marcus, legendary retailer and chairman emeritus of Neiman-Marcus, "What do the wealthy, powerful, and famous people you know have in common?"

"They all have 24-hour days," replied the man who counted many of these individuals as personal friends.

Then he explained: "The world has expanded in almost all directions, but we still have a 24-hour day. The most successful people and the most unsuccessful people all receive the same ration of hours each day."

The difference between being successful and not being successful depends on how you use your daily ration of 24 hours.

Time management has always been important. But it's more crucial today than ever before. Why?

- Because of the need to find a balance between career, family, and social life. More and more people are realizing that career is not enough.

- Because of the information explosion. It's impossible even to look at all the information that's available.

- Because of competitive pressures. A recent advertisement puts it thus: "He Who Hesitates Is Lunch."

- Because consumers—your customers and clients—want quality, and they want it now. They feel the same pressures that you do.

- Because a lot of money can be made by people who discover time-saving ways to do virtually anything in the marketplace.

ॐ

WHAT YOU CAN LEARN FROM
THIS BOOK

- *If you are in sales.*   Effective time tactics are absolutely critical in sales because so much of a salesperson's time is not closely supervised. Effective time tactics can help you meet quotas, earn bonuses, go to the President's Club. Effective use of your time will make or break your career.

- *If you are a manager.*   In today's fiercely competitive climate, managers often must compete with fewer people and still maintain quality. The projects that managers emphasize, how well they delegate, and to whom they delegate affect the bottom line and determine how effective their organizations are. You may be a "doer" manager; that is, you manage by doing more than anyone else and hope that others in your organization will follow your good example. This management philosophy eventually leads to burnout and an organization that stops when you stop.

- *If you are an executive.*   If your office is on the executive floor, you probably are already using some of the time tactics described in this book. But the most successful executives are always looking for new ways to streamline their efforts and become even more effective. This book can help you add to your personal repertoire. It also contains word tactics you can teach your support people in developing a time-conscious organizational culture.

- *If you are a student.*   If you can learn to manage your time, this ability will improve your grades, enable you to meet and develop new friends, help you have a richer social life. If you master these skills, they will help you land a good job when your school days are over.

- *If you are self-employed.*   It's a new world, without a supervisor. There's no time clock to punch. No one will tell you what you should be doing. Now it's up to you to use your time efficiently so that you can stay in business.

- *If you want to achieve balance in your life.*   You may already be engaged in the national pastime that involves finding a balance between the work you do and the life you live. One of the major trends in American society today is the growing awareness that a job is not all there is.

- *If you are overwhelmed by your work, with too much to do and not enough time to do it.*   Learn survival techniques from survivors.

WHAT IS THE BEST STRATEGY TO FOLLOW?

If you want to improve your life—whether you're starting a new career or learning how to manage your time better—there's one strategy to follow. It works flawlessly. That strategy is this: Study successful individuals and model what they do.

This book tells how very successful individuals manage their time. Many of the time tactics come from interviews that I conducted for radio, TV, newspapers, magazines, and books. Some of these individuals are famous, some are international figures. Others are not well known at all.

However, I make a distinction between being famous and being successful. A lot of people are successful who are not famous. Fame means that somebody has discovered you. A lot of successful people just haven't been discovered.

Some of the very best time tactics have come from people who are not famous. Many come from my workshops in which participants shared their ideas. They gave me workable tactics that they had refined in the laboratory of life.

I have tried to acknowledge the source of the tactics whenever possible. Sometimes I don't remember who told me about a particular tactic. Even if I did, I probably would discover that the person who told it to me was not its original creator. In this respect, I feel a bit like Abraham Lincoln who said he didn't create most of his famous stories. He said he was a *retailer* of ideas, not a wholesaler or a manufacturer.

Not every tactic will work for every reader, every personality, every situation. Some are contradictory. For example, one proven time tactic is to write your thank-you notes within 48 hours after the event. But one of the successful individuals in this book designates certain days of the month for catching up on matters like thank-you notes. She gets a remarkable amount of work done and manages not to offend people with her plan either. The time tactics should be thought of as possibilities, as options. It's your call, your choice, based on what will work for you.

Don't think that you have to make major, earth-shaking changes in your life in order to use time more effectively. Many people never attempt to improve their time management ability because they don't want to take the time to learn a complicated-looking system.

It's really easy, if you tackle one time tactic at a time. Try it out, and if it works, assimilate it into your everyday routine. Then go on to another one. You can do most anything if you take it on in small increments.

Try for just a 5 percent improvement. That works out to three minutes per hour. You will save that much time simply following the telephone tactics described in this book.

A 5 percent improvement will work wonders in an organization—if everyone does it. I tell the managers who send employees to my workshops, "If I can teach each participant to become 5 percent more efficient, and if you send 20 people, you will receive the equivalent of an additional employee at no additional cost—someone you won't have to interview, discipline, or ever fire."

Reading about other people's tactics can make your own life richer, give you new tools to work with.

Much has been written about time management, much of it very good. Several of the best ideas from the time-management literature are summarized in this book.

Some of the time tactics seem simple. But don't dismiss a time tactic just because it doesn't sound complicated or demanding. As you will learn later in the book, the head of one of the nation's largest steel companies saved thousands of dollars because he implemented one simple idea.

And don't dismiss a tactic because it isn't new. Often in the pursuit of important goals, we need reminders, not new information. Sometimes you simply need to reaffirm what you are already doing.

Whenever you can streamline a process or eliminate hassles and nuisances, you don't just save time. You make your life more pleasant.

Gloria Steinem once told me in an interview that many women never reach their goals because they keep waiting for someone to take charge of their lives. They do not seize the initiative themselves. As Steinem said that, I thought to myself, not just women are guilty. Men also need to understand what she's saying. Steinem concluded: "I've wasted an enormous amount of time, and time is life. Time is all there is."

Many years earlier Benjamin Franklin stated that same idea: "Dost thou love life? Then do not squander time, for time is the stuff life is made of."

B. Eugene Griessman

Acknowledgments

From my teenage years onward I have known that time is precious and have thought long and hard about how to use it wisely. Many individuals have been my teachers, some without knowing it.

Some of my teachers were very busy and often famous individuals with enormous demands on their time, yet they devoted some of their precious moments to do interviews with me. I will always be grateful.

Others helped me produce the book itself: Karen E. Shepherd, who was one of the first believers in the project; Mel Kranzberg, who continually provided inspiration and illustrations; Murray Brown, who patiently helped get the manuscript into presentable shape; Steve Walker, my former assistant who made wonderful suggestions, found resources, and provided valuable critiques; A. D. Van Nostrand and Joan Pettigrew, who organized the earliest draft so that it could be shown to a publisher; my friends in the Georgia Speakers Association—Dick Biggs, Terry Brock, Ken Futch, Austin McGonigle, Alf Nucifora, and Barbara Pagano—who worked their way through the manuscript, offered suggestions, and told me what the reading public would read; Jan Harris, who diligently looked after the book's best interests; Dan Ragsdale, a friend of many years who told McGraw-Hill my idea was a good one; Betsy Brown, who believed him and has guided the project brilliantly; Jane Palmieri, who carefully oversaw the book's production; and Jeannine Drew, a superb editor who crafted a clumsy and misshapen document into something that we now believe will prove valuable to many readers.

*Time Tactics of
Very Successful People*

es 1 *es*

Get a Handle on Your Time

es

THE MYTH OF "FREE" TIME

Taking time is a thief's trade; making time a strategist's. An effective manager must be both strategist and thief, stealing time from less compelling or more leisurely pursuits to get the job done. —LEWIS KELLY

Sometimes you will hear the comment, "Do that in your free time." What is usually meant is, "Do that when you aren't involved in something important." But the truth is, there is no such thing as free time. We may have *leisure* time, but no one has free time. You may be lying beside a pool or attending a play, but that's not free time. All time has value.

To make that point, a CEO of a large corporation brought a "money clock" into the executive meeting room. Attendees at meetings punched in. The clock, which was programmed with the hourly cost of each attendee, calculated the amount of time that was elapsing and the total cost of the meeting in dollars. The CEO made his point. Meetings that run on and on seem to be free, but they can be extremely costly.

It's far easier to think of tangible things like cars and houses as having value. Time, because it is invisible and intangible, doesn't get enough respect. If someone stole a painting or jewelry from

1

you, you would be upset and report the crime to the police. But the theft of time usually is not even considered a misdemeanor.

Unless you're a lawyer, accountant, or psychiatrist, it takes a certain amount of education to think of your own time as having value. Even if you bill clients by the hour, you may segregate that way of thinking into a neat compartment labeled "business." Away from work, you may not think of your time as valuable. An occasional glance at the chart below may help you realize how valuable even a minute of your time is.

WHAT IS YOUR TIME WORTH?*

If annually you earn	Every hour saved is worth	Every minute saved is worth	In a year one hour saved a day is worth
$ 30,000	$15.36	$.256	$ 3,750
35,000	17.93	.299	4,375
40,000	20.49	.342	5,000
45,000	23.05	.384	5,625
50,000	25.61	.427	6,250
55,000	28.17	.469	6,875
60,000	30.73	.512	7,500
65,000	33.29	.555	8,125
70,000	35.86	.598	8,750
75,000	38.42	.640	9,375
80,000	40.98	.683	10,000
85,000	43.54	.726	10,625
90,000	46.10	.768	11,250
95,000	48.66	.811	11,875
100,000	51.23	.854	12,250

*Based on 244 eight-hour working days per year.

SOURCE: Chart courtesy of Dictaphone Corporation. Used by permission.

This doesn't mean that you will have your eye on the clock every moment you're playing with your child or having a drink with a friend. What this chart does is help you realize how valuable your time is. None of it is free. When you're relaxing with family or friends or wandering through the woods on a stroll, you're investing some of your time or giving some away. That's what Stanley Marcus, the legendary CEO of Neiman-Marcus, meant when he told me, "I am miserly with my time in some areas so that I can be profligate with my time in other areas."

GIVE YOURSELF A RAISE

If you've accepted the basic idea that time has value, and more importantly, if you really understand that *your* time has value, you can do what time management expert Jeffrey Mayer recommends: Give yourself a raise. That's right. Put a price on your time. Then raise that price.

What is your time really worth? If you were able to market yourself at the rate that your most-developed skills can command, how much would someone pay you? Let's assume for a moment that you earn $50,000 a year. Look at the chart. Every hour of your time is worth $25.61. Every minute is worth $0.427.

Whatever your time is now worth in the marketplace, double it. If you're presently earning $25 an hour, you are now worth $50 an hour. If you're already making $50 an hour, you are now worth $100.

Don't dismiss this thinking exercise as unimportant. *The way you think about time and think about yourself will affect everything that happens to you the rest of your life.* It's just like playing golf. The game is won or lost in your head.

If you begin to think of your time as actually being worth quite a large sum of money, don't be surprised if before long you are actually making this kind of money. What will happen is that you will begin to realize the cost of an hour frittered away. Then you will start looking for ways to cut down on waste caused by inefficiencies. And, perhaps most importantly, if your time is really worth $100 or $200 or $300 an hour, you will begin to pick and choose more carefully the projects and requests that come to you.

These numbers are hypothetical. The point of this exercise is not to become crassly materialistic about your time, but to emphasize that your time is precious.

Whatever your present value per hour, double it or triple it. Then, invest your high-priced hours deliberately. Don't give them away unless you choose to. And don't consider that everybody else's time is more valuable than your own.

BILL YOURSELF: A TACTIC THAT PROFESSIONALS USE TO BECOME MORE EFFICIENT

Lawrence H. Summers is now United States Secretary of Treasury. Previously he was with the World Bank, where he was chief economist with a research staff of some 600 people. Prior to that he was a professor at Harvard University in the economics department.

When I told Summers that I was writing a book on time management, he shared this tactic with me. He told me that when he was teaching at Harvard and encountered students who were having trouble getting their work done, he asked them to keep a log of their time—the way lawyers and accountants do. If they actually worked 30 minutes on a project, they logged in 30 minutes. No more. No less. He told them to log only what they could ethically bill a client. If they took out time for a snack break, that time was to be deducted from the log. Using the log, students realized that they often imagined that they were working longer on projects than they actually were.

This tactic probably isn't necessary for people who have learned to manage their time well. But for the person who's having trouble managing time, keeping a log can be a useful diagnostic tool. A log can have shock value even for experienced workers when they see how much time is simply unaccounted for.

Some seasoned time tacticians use logs not just for shock value, but regularly as a self-management tool. James L. S. Collins, president of Chick-fil-A, has been logging himself for years. He started doing it as a discipline, and found the practice so useful that he's never abandoned it.

Many attorneys and accountants live most of their working hours with a log in front of them. When I asked a highly successful attorney what it's like to live that way, he replied: "You get used to it. You learn to just jot down when you start a phone conversation and when you end it. After a while, it's a way of life."

Keeping a log isn't for everyone. Many people who are excellent time managers wouldn't think of keeping one. The last thing they want is more paperwork. I have occasionally kept a log for a short period of time simply to see how I was doing, but I don't do it on a regular basis.

You may want to try keeping a log at least for a brief interval. If you do it honestly and carefully, you will know exactly what you're spending your time doing. A log doesn't leave much room for self-delusion.

❧ 2 ❧

Get Organized

❧
SET YOUR PRIORITIES

All the high achievers I know establish priorities. Helen Gurley Brown, editor of *Cosmopolitan,* keeps a copy of the magazine on her desk at all times. Whenever she's tempted to fritter away time doing some activity that doesn't directly contribute to the well-being of the magazine, a glance at the magazine helps her get back on track.

Brown says that unless you have a sense of priorities, you may work very hard and even be self-congratulatory at the end of the day, but you will be farther from attaining your goal than when you started.

Knowing that all items on your to-do list are not equal and shouldn't be treated as equals is essential. This is where many would-be time tacticians go astray. They dutifully create a to-do list, but when they begin to execute the items on the list, they treat them all alike.

There are several ways to designate which items are most important. One way is to limit the number. Another way is to create two lists—a short-term checklist and a long-term, top-priority list. Some individuals put asterisks, or the letters *A, B, C,* or the numbers 1, 2, 3 beside the most important items. Each system has merit.

How do you decide which tasks or meetings go on the short list or which get the asterisks, the ones, or the *A*'s? One way is to subject the prospective candidates for your list to some intensive questioning. Here are some questions to use for the grilling:

- Will it help me reach some important goal in my life?
- Does it have a deadline—a real deadline, like April 15?
- Is it an *order* from someone I can't ignore, like a supervisor or a commanding officer?
- Does it involve doing what my work or business is all about?
- Will doing it advance my career, or conversely, will *not* doing it hinder my career?
- Will it make me more knowledgeable, help me fulfill my potential?
- Will it require coordinated efforts with others? If so, can I get those people started on their parts of the project right away? Then can I turn my attention to something that doesn't require their input?
- Is it important to someone I really care about?
- Will it matter a year from now?
- Will it really matter if I don't do it?

If the task in question doesn't elicit a yes from *any* of the questions listed above, it doesn't deserve top priority.

In planning a day's activities, you may not be able to tackle a number-one task the first thing in the morning. But you may be able to make some number-two phone calls. You can drop off laundry on the way to the office—a number-three item—before you make a very important phone call to the west coast—a number-one item.

Developing a plan for *when* you do the number-one items isn't as important as knowing what your number-one items are. Getting to them then becomes a matter of creating a system and working your system. "If you can tell where you want to go," an old proverb states, "somebody will be able to tell you how to get there."

❧
WRITE DOWN YOUR GOALS

The most important question to ask about your priorities is the first question on the list: "Will doing this help me reach some important goal in my life?" The legendary hotelier Conrad Hilton attributed his career success to the power of a goal. But Hilton did more than write down his top priority. Here's the story.

The great depression was not kind to Hilton. After the crash of 1929, people weren't traveling, and if they were, they weren't staying in the hotels Hilton had acquired during the boom years of the 1920s. By 1931, his creditors were threatening to foreclose, his laundry was in hock, and he was borrowing money from a bellboy so he could eat. That year Conrad Hilton came upon a photograph of the Waldorf Hotel, with its 6 kitchens, 200 cooks, 500 waiters, 2000 rooms, and its private hospital and private railroad siding in the basement. Hilton clipped that photograph out of the magazine, and wrote across it, "The Greatest of Them All."

The year 1931 was "a presumptuous, an outrageous time to dream," Hilton later wrote. But he put the photo of the Waldorf in his wallet, and when he had a desk again, slipped the picture under the glass top. From then on, it was always in front of him. As he worked his way back up and acquired new bigger desks, he would slip the cherished photo under the glass. Eighteen years later, in October 1949, Conrad Hilton acquired the Waldorf.

That picture gave Hilton's dream shape and substance. There was something for his mind to focus upon. It became a cue for behavior, serving the same function as Helen Gurley Brown's magazine that she always keeps on her desk.

I never met Conrad Hilton, but I do know someone whose career has been similarly transformed by goals. His name is Homer C. Rice, long-time athletic director of the Georgia Tech Yellow Jackets. Rice has been so successful that his peers in the National Association of Collegiate Athletic Directors annually confer an award named for him on the nation's top athletic director.

Rice began his coaching career at a rural high school in Kentucky. He eventually moved to a larger high school, where he compiled an incredible win-loss-tie record of 101–9–7, with seven undefeated seasons, a 50-game undefeated streak, and five straight championship years. He subsequently became a university coach, a professional coach, and a university athletic director.

How did he do it? Rice began to read all the books he could find on achievement. He observed that many of those books recommended writing down what you want to attain—your aspirations, your goals, your dreams. The young Kentucky coach began to do just that, and he wrote beside the goals the dates for attainment, plus a plan for achieving them. One by one, almost by magic, Rice began to reach the goals he had written down. He was so pleased with the outcome that he began to teach his players to do the same. He still does.

When I taught management classes at Georgia Tech, I sometimes invited Rice to make a presentation. The last time I had him do it, he showed us a set of 3 × 5 cards. Then he said, "These are my goals—one on each card. I take them with me everywhere. When I'm at the airport waiting for a plane, I'll pull them out and begin to read them. The real fun is expecting them to happen."

He believes goals should be written clearly and concisely. Reading the goals aloud at least twice each day helps imprint the goals on the unconscious mind. "Be patient, be relaxed, be confident," he says. "If you deserve what you are asking for, it will come to you."

Lewis J. Walker, former national president of the Institute of Certified Financial Planners, was asked by a newspaper reporter recently to describe the fundamentals of a sound investment program. They chatted for awhile and finally the reporter asked, "What keeps people from being successful?"

Walker replied, "Fuzzy goals."

The reporter asked Walker to explain what he meant by fuzzy goals. He replied, "A few minutes ago, I asked *you* what your goals were, and you replied that you wanted to have a cabin in the mountains someday. That was a fuzzy goal. *Someday* is the problem."

"Your goal isn't specific," Walker told her. "And because it isn't specific, it's not very likely to happen. If you truly want a cabin in the mountains, you will need to go find the mountain, find out how much that cabin that you want costs today, and with inflation, how much it will cost, say, five years from now. Then you will need to determine how much you'll need to save per month to realize that goal. If you do that, you probably will have a cabin in the mountains. If you don't, it probably won't happen." Dreams can be delightful. But fuzzy dreams, uncoupled from an action plan, are delusions. They are rusting boxcars on a sidetrack.

Walker says if you want to have a million dollars by the time you're 65, and you're 30 years of age, you can have that if you will simply put back about $90 a month and let it compound. Or, Walker says, you can *hope* to have a million dollars one day. If you don't do anything specific about it, you can count on the lottery.

🙌
APPLY THE 80/20 RULE

In deciding on your priorities—what to do, what not to do, and when to do what—one test to apply is what has become known as "the 80/20 rule." Here's what happened to William E. Moore when he tried it.

When Moore graduated from college in 1939, he took a job as salesman for the Glidden Paint Company. His draw was $160 per month. Moore set a goal: $1000 a month. As soon as he had a good feel for his job, Moore sat down with his client information and sales charts and determined exactly who accounted for most of his business. He found that approximately 20 percent of his customers accounted for 80 percent of his sales. He also realized that he was spending equal amounts of time with each of his customers, regardless of how much they purchased.

What Bill Moore did next was to return 36 of his *least* active customers to the company and focus only on the top 20 percent of his customers. The 80/20 rule became Moore's magic formula. What happened? He met his goal of $1000 per month the first year, surpassed it the next, and went on to become the top producer on the west coast. Never abandoning the rule, Moore became a very wealthy man, eventually becoming chairman of the Kelly-Moore Paint Company.

When I mentioned this concept in a time tactics workshop recently, a prominent jewelry wholesaler pulled out his sales figures for the previous year to see if the 80/20 rule applied to his business. Sure enough, his top 3000 customers—26 percent of his customers—accounted for 80 percent of his business. In his case, the 80/20 rule was not exact. It was off by 6 percent. Twenty-six percent of his customers accounted for 80 percent of his business.

What about the customers at the bottom? "We've wrestled with this problem for years," he told me. "The bottom 20 percent actually cost us money. Our customers are jewelry stores. We mail them catalogs and other promotional materials, hoping they will increase the size of their orders. Maybe we should do what Bill Moore did and spend our energy cultivating the ones at the top."

His sales figures demonstrate that the 80/20 rule is only a rough approximation, but a good guide. In many activities, the ratio will be higher; in others, it will be lower. It's not a scientific law, but it is one way to make decisions about whether a task is high priority or even worth doing.

You can apply the principle of the 80/20 rule to customers you call on or to the items on your to-do list. Paying attention to what will get the greatest return sets you free from those tasks that contribute little or nothing to your success. Like Bill Moore, you may need to "fire" 80 percent of your customers, eliminate 80 percent of what you've been putting on your to-do list.

CREATE A TO-DO LIST THAT WORKS, AND WORK YOUR LIST

Don't try to remember everything: Write it down.

Make sure your next day's tasks are written down before the light goes out. There are several good reasons why this is good advice:

- If the tasks are written down, you can sleep more soundly. Otherwise your mind may disturb you all night long with the message: "Don't forget. Don't forget. Don't forget." It is mentally tiring trying not to forget.

- If the tasks are written down, your mind is freed to solve problems, not just remember them. It's amazing what the unconscious mind can do if you let it work on problems. The brain works like a parallel processor, doing foreground tasks and background tasks simultaneously. Once you write something down, your brain can transfer it to a background task and start working on the problem even though you're not consciously aware of it.

- If the tasks are written down, you have taken a step toward commitment. If a task is not worth writing down, it's probably not worth doing.

Make your list comprehensive.

Don't rely on reminders scribbled on scraps of paper here and there. Don't rely on Post-its on your desk or held in place by magnets on the refrigerator. If your reminders are scattered here and there, you have created lots of cracks for things to fall through.

Be sure there is at least one place where all the items can be found and checked off. It may in an organizer that you carry with you or in a computer. Whatever the format, keep it current and make sure it's available to you at all times.

If you must, use Post-its and scribbled notes as extra reminders, but don't let them become your main system. If you do, you are inviting a major blunder.

If your list is combined with an appointment book, it's prudent to keep one copy in your office or on your main computer, just in case the other one is lost or stolen. The office copy will need to be updated daily. This bit of redundancy can pay off handsomely. (See "Develop Survival Skills If You're Absentminded" in Chapter 9.)

Check your list regularly.

Periodically review your list. Look at it first thing in the morning, without fail. If you make sure that everything that you intend to do gets on your comprehensive list—and if you check that list regularly—there is no way that anything will ever fail to be done just because you forgot about it. Malcolm Forbes, Jr., keeps a sheet of paper with his top items on his desk continually. Forbes says this sheet of paper is the core of his personal management system. "Whenever I feel I'm getting bogged down, I just look at that sheet and see whether what I'm bogged down on is what I should be bogged down on." Forbes typically will have some 20 items on the sheet: phone calls, to letters, to a small column for editorials that he has to dictate. He told me, "If you don't have a constant reminder of things you would like to get done, they aren't going to get done."

It's also a powerful technique to use in managing others. Whenever the people who report to you are given assignments, make sure that they keep a list of the items assigned to them. In your subsequent meetings with them, ask them to bring the list with them to meetings and use it as the basis of their progress report. If you use the list this way, you will be sure that something delegated is not forgotten.

Few qualities are more important in business or in social situations than dependability. (I must admit that I have known a few individuals who deviously but successfully encouraged people to believe that they were absentminded and disorganized so that they could conveniently "forget" what they did not want to do.) Managers like to be able to delegate tasks and turn their attention to something else. People who plan meetings or social events like to know that if you made an agreement to participate, that you won't forget about it.

Limit the items on your list.

Your list should be comprehensive, but it shouldn't be encyclopedic. You can commit to too much.

Mary Kay Ash, known to the world as Mary Kay, told me that years before she founded her cosmetics company, she heard an anecdote about Charles Schwab, who at the time was the president of one of the nation's big steel companies. He was approached by Ivy Lee, a management consultant, who said to him, "I can tell you how to make your company more efficient."

Charles Schwab replied, "How much will it cost?"

Lee answered, "Nothing, if it doesn't work. But if it does work, I'll expect you to pay a percentage of the money your company saves because of the idea."

"That seems fair," Schwab stated, and asked what needed to be done. "I'll need to spend 10 minutes one-on-one with each of your top executives. Schwab agreed, and Lee began to meet with the executives. He told each of them: "At the end of the day, before you leave the office, write down six things that you didn't get done today that you really need to do tomorrow."

The executives agreed to the idea. As they began to execute the plan, they found that they were becoming more focused. They worked hard at the items on the list because they had created the list. Soon there was a noticeable improvement in the productivity of the company. It was so impressive that a few months later Schwab wrote Lee a check for $35,000.

Mary Kay told me, "When I heard that story, I thought to myself, if it was worth $35,000 to Charles Schwab, then it's worth $35,000 to Mary Kay." So, at the end of each day, she began to write down the six most important things she would do tomorrow. And she began to urge her sales associates to do the same.

Today Mary Kay Cosmetics—which now has some 200,000 sales associates—prints little pink note pads by the millions. At the top of each sheet are the words, "The Six Most Important Things I Must Do Tomorrow."

Assign a date and time for the items on your list.

Harold L. Taylor, one of the premier time management consultants in the world, doesn't believe in time logs and feels that to-do lists—as used by most people—become tools for procrastination.

Taylor believes that you must make a commitment to do what's on the list. The best way to make a commitment is to give each task on the list *a specific time slot.*

Most people use their planning diaries just to put down meetings and appointments. Taylor uses his planning diary—which is broken down into half-hour increments—to schedule his tasks as well as appointments.

If you put only people and meetings on your planner, when someone calls and wants to meet with you, say, next Tuesday, and if nothing is written down, the entire day seems to be available. That's a big mistake, Taylor believes. Important tasks should be logged in as well as people and meetings: "Not until I started scheduling tasks for a specific time slot in my planning calendar did I succeed in actually getting the jobs done."

"Don't give people free access to your time," Taylor adds. When someone calls for an appointment next Tuesday, and you are scheduled from 8:00 until 9:30 that day to write an important proposal, suggest a 9:30 meeting—but not until you ask what the person wants to talk about. You may be able to settle the matter on the phone. "And don't be afraid to set a time limit," Taylor advises. "A simple, 'How long do you think it will take us?'" will suffice.

If you're a manager, consider creating to-do lists for your people.

Like most successful executives, Susan Taylor, editor-in-chief of *Essence* magazine, is a listmaker. She prepares to-do lists for herself *and* for some of her associates as well. Often Taylor goes away to a New England retreat on weekends. There she thinks about projects, looks at articles, and works through concepts. When she returns on Monday, she often has to-do lists for her key people, with assignments for each of them. The priority items get red checks; the highest priority, two red checks. Often, information needed to carry out a task, like a business card or a background letter, will be attached to the to-do list.

A manager who attended one of my workshops uses a magnetic board for his unit's to-do list. He says the magnetic board allows the priorities to be changed if necessary, and it permits other people to see how he rates a project's importance.

Create a long-term list.

Many time tacticians work out a long-term list. When I spoke at a national sales conference recently, I made it a point to speak to the salesperson who was number one in the company. I asked him what tactic was most valuable to him. He replied: "My *monthly* to-do list." He explained that he knows a month in advance most of the key calls that he would make.

Some individuals even estimate the amount of time each of the projects on their long-term list will require for completion. They then use these weekly, monthly, or even yearly lists to generate their daily lists.

Debera J. Salam, editor-in-chief of *Payroll Practitioner's Monthly,* arranges her months and years like they are a filing cabinet. The first two weeks of the month are devoted to writing newsletters. "I don't accept speaking engagements during the first two weeks of the month unless it is a great opportunity," Salam told me. "If I do accept something during this period, I take my laptop computer so that I can do work away from the office." The third and fourth weeks are dedicated to other activities, like speaking appearances. The end of the month is the time when she catches up on thank-you notes, does networking, and plans for the future. She plans her year in advance. Some months are for writing books, some months are seminar months. One or two months are dedicated to new ventures. Using this approach, Salam has been able to produce an amazing amount of material and maintain a large and devoted following in her field.

3

Increase Your Efficiency

NEATNESS IS MORE THAN A NEUROTIC COMPULSION

Charles Schulz's desk at One Snoopy Lane, Santa Rosa, California, was clean and the tools of his craft were arranged in perfect order the day I visited him. Somehow I had expected a studio in disarray, but I was badly mistaken. When I commented on it, the creator of "Peanuts" replied: "I like things neat."

What we call *neat*, the British call *tidy*. We don't use either word very much. They sound a bit juvenile, words to describe a kindergarten or a child's room. They even sound a bit obsessive, a little neurotic.

Despite the negative connotations of *tidy* or *neat*, arranging things in an orderly manner can be a powerful time tactic. Often it's not that much extra trouble either. You have to put whatever you're using *somewhere* when you're finished, so why not put it back where you can find it easily the next time you need it? Why leave dishes in the sink when you can put them in the dishwasher? They have to go there eventually.

Have you ever watched master auto mechanics work? Notice where their tools are—carefully set out in trays, all lined up ready for use. When they're at work, they try not to look away from the engine or the part they're repairing. They don't want to lose their concentration. They reach out for the tool, and know

17

where to find it. And when they're finished, they make sure that it is put back in its place.

The same principle works in other fields too. When I was a college student, I briefly held a job as a spreader in a textile plant. In those days, spreaders pushed carts that were laden with bolts of cloth down long platforms. We would spread the cloth in long rows, one layer upon the other. As soon as the cart was empty, we would get another bolt of cloth and put it on the cart. When the pile was several hundred layers of cloth high, a paper pattern was spread on the top layer of the pile. Then the cutters would cut out the patterns.

I worked at night, after the school day was finished. One evening, the owner happened to come into the building and watched us at our work. His name was Mr. Stone. Nobody I knew called him by his first name or even knew what it was. But everybody knew that he was very successful and very rich.

We had been a bit careless prior to his arrival, and had tossed the bolts of cloth in a jumbled heap near the platform. Mr. Stone walked over to where we were working, and began straightening them up, placing them in neat rows. After a few minutes, he told us to stop what we were doing and restack the rest of them ourselves. When we finished, he gave us a little lecture that I never forgot. Mr. Stone told us never to let sloppiness begin, even in a small way. Once sloppiness began, he said, it would spread throughout the building. Eventually the whole plant would be a mess.

I thought of that lecture years later when I talked with Robert Prather, the man who helped J. B. Fuqua acquire numerous companies for a multi-billion-dollar conglomerate. Prather told me that neatness was one thing he looked for when he considered buying a company. He said if a building looked messy and unorganized, it usually was an indication that other things in the company were not being attended to. For him, untidiness was a warning sign not to buy.

John Williams, a prominent real estate developer, told me he can always tell the caliber of a new building by the appearance of the construction site. Is it clean? Are the building materials stacked carefully? Management consultant Alf Nucifora says he can instantly tell a lot about a company by the cleanliness of its lobby. Are the carpets soiled, is the paint and wallpaper scratched, are the magazines old, are the ashtrays full?

Not every high achiever is tidy. In fact, perhaps the most prolific creative person I know—renowned historian Mel Kranzberg—has the most unbelievably jumbled office and desk I have ever seen. Kranzberg has a lot of good company. Throughout history, many great achievers have been anything but tidy. We might speculate that they would have achieved much more if they had been tidier, but that's like speculating whether Caruso would have sung better if he had taken voice lessons. We simply don't know.

Clearly, neatness is a time tactic that works for some but is not essential for others. As far as you are concerned, paying more attention to order and neatness won't hurt you, and just might pay huge dividends. A significant number of highly effective people, like Mr. Stone, have learned that neatness can do wonders for efficiency as well as the bottom line.

⁊⬤

MAKE YOUR WORKPLACE WORK

Anita Corey, who's president of CHS Planning and Design Corporation in New York City, has observed that companies often spend lavishly on the reception area, the conference rooms, and the executive offices—the places where clients might be invited, but they skimp on the places where the work force produces the service or goods. "It's the wrong emphasis," Corey says. "Most people who earn $40,000 a year believe it's OK to buy a $20,000 car which lasts for four years. They'll spend two or three hours a day in a car that has an ergonomically correct seat allowing for changes in the angle of the back, changes in height, and changes in the distance from the seat to the pedals and steering. An office chair in which we spend eight hours a day seldom costs more than $300, and has none of these adjustments. An $800 chair will."

Most of us spend a lot of time in a place devoted to work. Even people who work in outside sales come back to a desk or office from time to time. So it makes sense to pay attention to the place where you do your work. A few changes might pay huge dividends.

- *Give thought to how the parts of your workplace are configured.* If the space itself does not fit the flow of your daily work, making a change may save several hundred extra steps per day, thousands per year. Extra steps mean wasted time and energy. A rearrangement of vital equipment, storage space, your desk, and your phone can mean big time savings. You may need expert advice from a consultant who specializes in office and workspace design. This expert can make a positive difference in your bottom line, by spending time with you, studying the work flow, and rearranging your space and equipment.

- *Don't be afraid to spend money.* Purchase everything you need to be efficient. The purchase of an inexpensive gadget or tool may save many hours—a minute or two a day. Maintain what you have in such a way that you get maximum mileage from them.

- *Don't use the top of your desk for storage.* First, the contrary view. There are some very successful people who deliberately violate this rule. Alan Weiss, author of *Million Dollar Consulting,* is one of them. He sorts incoming materials into stacks. One stack is for urgent materials, like letters that need to be dealt with immediately and reports that need to be written at once. One stack contains items that require some thought or that can be set aside for prompt but not immediate action. The third is reading material and other items that can be looked at later. When he sets out on a trip, he will grab items from the third stack to read on the plane. Weiss likes to keep the stacks in front of him, not out of the way in a file drawer somewhere. He says it does good things for him psychologically to cut down the size of the stack.

   That plan works well for Weiss, and I must admit that materials tend to "stack up" in my workspace. In general, however, I find it best to follow the principle of the clean desk. It gives me a good feeling to keep it clear and ready for action. A desktop is prime workspace and should contain only those items that you use every day. A cluttered desk doesn't necessarily mean a creative mind. It may simply be a sign of disorganization and lack of focus. Space-management consultant Greg Vetter says every piece of paper on the top of your desk is a decision you haven't made.

Many highly efficient and effective people try to have only one thing on the desk at once. Stacks of paper are kept off the desk except when they are being dealt with, because any clutter can create a degree of stress. The less there is to distract you, the greater your chances of giving the task at hand a high level of concentration.

In large companies, the cleanest desks tend to belong to the people who are highest in the organization. In fact, there is an element of snob appeal associated with a clean desk. Often it is the "worker bees" who have cluttered desks. Executives and senior managers don't. Some image consultants recommend a clean desk for that reason alone. Bill Marriott told me that his father always believed in having a clean desk. "One day we discovered that the way he had a clean desk was just to dump everything in a drawer."

However, a clean desk is more than a status symbol. The material that you are storing on your desk can readily be transferred to files. Here are some rules the experts recommend to organize your materials and keep yourself organized:

1. *Use the accessibility principle.*   Organize your material by asking: What do I use every day? Every week? Every month? Every year? Never? The answers to these questions tell you where to put what.

   What you use every day should be placed close at hand, perhaps in the drawers of your desk. Items that are looked at every month or every year should not be in your desk, but in file cabinets or storage boxes. It makes no sense to keep file folders full of old letters in your desk if you never look at them. If you will never read them again, toss them.

2. *Create a "To Be Filed" folder.*   As you go through this sorting exercise, you will encounter items that you haven't decided how to deal with. Pull these items together in a folder that can be marked "To Be Filed."

3. *Create a "To Do" folder.*   Instead of stacking items on your desk or credenza, keep them in a drawer close to you that

you can readily access. You may even create two such folders, based on the importance of the items. I personally have one such folder labeled "1" and another labeled "2."

4. *Regularly schedule time for catching up, reorganizing, working your way through your folders.* If you've been out of town on trips or working on items that have close deadlines, your folders may be bulging with material. For an hour or two, do what needs to be done to keep the system working. Toss out what seemed important when you first set it aside but isn't important anymore. You'll discover to your delight that some of the things you wondered about doing have solved themselves without any action on your part.

ৼ৶

LEARN TO RELY ON CHECKLISTS

Time management consultant Merrill Douglass recommends using a checklist (this is different from the to-do list) for recurring activities. If you are a frequent traveler, keep a list of the items that will be needed on the trip: essential articles of clothing and accessories, business cards, and so on. The checklist stays permanently in the suitcase. That way, you don't arrive without hair dryer, business cards, handkerchief, nail clippers, and so on. It's a time-saver and a grief preventer. Some people call the checklist a "quick sheet." They use it to write down essential items, tips, shortcuts, and reminders for meetings and parties—in fact, for any routine.

The checklist can be useful even for certain tasks that you don't do regularly. For example, a checklist showing how to use the copier can be displayed prominently near the copying machine or attached to it. Such a list will avoid waste and save time. People who use the machine day in and day out won't need it, but the occasional user—like an executive when the assistant is sick—will avoid wasting paper and time using a trial-and-error approach if a checklist is available.

Telemarketing consultant David Yoho, Jr., uses a checklist of questions to ask over the phone: "The form I use is better than I am," he says. "It assures me that I get the essential information that I want. What has made me very good through the years is using this form."

One of the best examples of the checklist is Harvey Mackay's 66-question customer profile, which he calls the "Mackay 66." The form has questions about Mackay's regular customers—their family, business background, schooling, special interests, hobbies, and the like.

Mackay requires that his people update the form continually. If a secretary sees something in the newspaper about one of their top customers, the information goes into the file. Just having the form available provides a reminder to pick up on vital information customers are willing to share, cues they are giving.

Mackay says using the checklist provides the salespeople and the company with lots of benefits. Salespeople and managers use the checklist to develop strategies for working with customers and clients. It also becomes the core of a permanent database about customers and clients that survives if individual salespeople move on to other jobs.

TAKE A CHECKRIDE: SEE YOURSELF AS OTHERS SEE YOU

Twice a year every commercial pilot in the United States is required to take a checkride. The purpose of the checkride is to determine if the pilot has begun to drift into bad habits.

The checkride doesn't determine whether or not the pilots are competent. That's already been established. The pilots of major airlines are superbly trained. The checkride makes sure that they stay at peak form.

There are scores of fields in which top people use the principle of the checkride. Some occupations require it for continued licensing or certification.

The checkride is an institutionalized part of many organizational cultures. The sales force at Merck Sharp and Dohme—the pharmaceutical marketing organization that consistently receives top rank in surveys of sales forces—puts recruits through an expensive, intensive yearlong training program. But the testing doesn't end at graduation. Employees are tested continuously. If they fail to score higher than 90 percent on three test scores, they are no longer employed. Even veteran sales representatives receive three to five weeks of training each year and are tested quarterly.[1]

Federal Express is another well-run company that uses the checkride principle. Employees who have direct contact with the public are tested on job knowledge every six months.

One of my colleagues who's a top national speaker invites a consultant to sit in on his presentations every six months or so. He asks him to listen for bad habits, for sloppy work. I use the tactic by asking my administrative assistant to offer suggestions about how I or he or we can perform our tasks in a more efficient manner. And I always try to get feedback on my public presentations by asking someone whose opinion I value to tell me what I could have done to make the presentation better.

Many sales organizations use consultants or their own people to go on calls with sales reps. The outsider-insider perspective can help the people performing the task to back away and think about how they can do it better.

Several years ago, after I had been chosen as a department head at a large university, I invited IBM consultants to evaluate our office procedures. The consultants studied what each of the secretaries did and asked them to keep time logs over a period of two or three weeks. This enabled the consultants to form a clear picture of the flow of work. Then they made their recommendations. As you might expect, they recommended that we purchase IBM equipment. (We did, and were pleased with the choice. It was an early version of a word processor, called a magnetic card typewriter.)

But, more importantly, these consultants also made some suggestions about other activities that were taking place in the office. As a result of their recommendations, we made several changes, which made our office run much more smoothly and efficiently.

You can do a checkride by using an audiotape or a videotape recorder. Rodney Dangerfield is one of many top entertainers who tape their presentations to hear audience reactions and improve their timing. You may not be an entertainer, but you can tape yourself as you make a sales presentation, conduct a meeting, or give a speech. (Even a mirror can do wonders.) Just seeing yourself the way others do can be an important step in attaining the image that you want to project.

When you are taped for the first time, you'll probably be shocked and discouraged at what you hear and see. But don't be too hard on yourself. Choose areas to improve only during the second or third viewings, not the first. The first viewing can be too much of a shock for you to be constructive about it.

If you are interested in being your very best, don't wait for some higher power to reveal it to you. Make it your business to find out. Take checkrides regularly, whether you have to or not.

BECOME A SPEED LEARNER

Just think of the time you have spent studying for exams of one sort or another. If you could learn more quickly, and afterward recall what you learned when you needed to, wouldn't that be a terrific time tactic? Absolutely.

Are there ways to learn more efficiently, more rapidly? The experts say yes. They say that you can dramatically increase your learning ability by using certain learning techniques and exercises.

There's no way to take all the work out of learning, but some of the techniques that learning experts recommend make learning easier, quicker, and more fun:

- *Drills and routines.* Whenever I've learned a foreign language, I've found that flash cards—with the foreign word on one side and the English on the other—helped me immensely. I frankly don't remember who it was who told me about the practice, but I soon was carrying a little pack with me and would practice at odd times. When I learned all the words in a pack, I would replace the old cards with new ones. The flash-card tactic can be used to learn all kinds of materials, not just a foreign language vocabulary.

   Just writing something down over and over can help fix material in the mind. It's a simple technique that's been used for millennia, but it still works. Use a pen or pencil and inexpensive paper, a chalk and chalkboard, or a computer.

■ *Visualization exercises.*   After you have put yourself into a receptive state, visualize yourself studying your chosen subject in an effective manner. Picture exactly where you will be studying. Imagine that you are feeling very interested as you explore the topic. See yourself mastering material.

   Follow through by actually doing what you have visualized. Some visualization coaches suggest that you practice this exercise just prior to falling asleep. The positive images that you create just prior to drifting off to sleep will influence how you respond during your waking hours. The looking-forward exercise actually prepares you mentally to take on these specific concepts. The best book I know on visualization is *Seeing with the Mind's Eye: The History, Techniques and Uses of Visualization* by Mike Samuels and Nancy Samuels (Random House, 1986).

■ *Multisensory learning.*   If you are studying the French language, you can create a learning environment around you that is French. Bring into that environment as many sights, sounds, tastes, and aromas of France as you can find. Bombard the senses. The more of your senses that you can involve in the learning experience, the more rapidly you will learn and the longer you will retain what you've learned.

■ *Dream learning.*   Some experts recommend that as you drift off to sleep each evening over a period of perhaps 30 days, focus your thoughts on aspects of material that you found to be fascinating or confusing. Affirm that you will process the new information subconsciously. Many individuals who have used this technique report that they solve problems or gain fresh insights.

■ *Music.*   It long has been recognized that certain kinds of music can have a calming effect on listeners. Other kinds of music can serve as a stimulant. Can music help learning? Yes, according to a recent experiment with college students at the University of California at Irvine. The study results indicated that listening to music improves performance in intelligence tests taken immediately afterward. The music the students listened to, incidentally, was piano sonatas by Mozart. Whether all music has the same effect or the improvement can be made permanent has not been determined. The researchers speculated that listening to music like Mozart's may stimulate neural pathways that are important to cognition.

- *Overviews.* If you're studying material that's already well organized in written form, look first at the organizational framework of the chapter or the book before you begin to look at specific paragraphs or sentences. Whenever you get a new book, look for compact statements of what the book is about. You may find this in a paragraph or two on the book jacket or in the introduction. Then look at the way the book is organized in the table of contents.

- *Selectivity.* People are not likely to learn unless their interest has been aroused. They are not going to continue to learn unless it is enjoyable, unless they perceive that it will be useful to them, or unless they realize that it will be painful if they don't. We gritted our teeth and learned the multiplication tables, not because it was fun, but because we knew it would be painful if we didn't. I learned how to use the computer because someone convinced me it would be useful later on.

Our likes and dislikes determine what we learn, how rapidly we learn, how much we learn, and how long we remember. Research on what is called the "selective processes" indicates that people try not to expose themselves to information they don't think will be useful or interesting or will run counter to their biases. If they are exposed to such information accidentally or against their wills, they tend to interpret it in such a way that the information will be distorted to suit their previous opinions. If they don't interpret it selectively or distort it, then they forget it.

❧ 4 ❧

Shortcuts

❧
READING SHORTCUTS

A shortcut isn't necessarily a short circuit. It makes perfectly good sense to avoid useless effort, needless redundancy. (Some redundancy, as we shall see, can be efficient.) Because so much effort is devoted to reading in our information-rich world, it's important to know how to read certain kinds of material quickly and efficiently, and some material not at all.

❧
SPEED READING

There are several good books on the subject, and speed-reading courses are available in many locations and on cassette. One of the best brief summaries of speed-reading principles is available in *CareerTracking: Twenty-Six Success Shortcuts to the Top* by CareerTrack founders Jimmy Calano and Jeff Salzman. Here are some of the most important tips that they recommend:

- *Set some speed-reading goals for yourself.* The brain is capable of processing well over 1000 words per minute, but the average reading speed is only about 250 words per minute. Many people chug along at 50 or 100 words per minute. In order to attain higher rates, find out where you are now. Clock yourself for one minute as you read some nonfiction book of average difficulty. Periodically recheck your rate to see how much progress you're making.

- *Be aware of your eye movements.* The eyes of slow readers stop as many as 10 times per line, whereas speed readers stop only two or three times per line. Try to increase the number of words you take in at each stop and move your eyes faster from stop to stop.

- *Don't read every word.* Learn to read thoughts, or complete ideas, not words.

- *Don't move your lips, even in your mind.* Slow readers "say" each word in their mind.

- *Keep going.* Resist the tendency to return to previously covered territory unless you are certain that you missed something really important.[2]

Cautions: Speed for speed's sake is not a desirable goal. Technical and scientific material may need to be read and reread. If you are an investor, you may want to pore over certain parts of the annual reports, especially the footnotes, much like a detective examining evidence at the scene of a crime. Some parts of an annual report are smoke and mirrors. Zip through this. If you are reading poetry, you may want savor a passage by reading every word aloud. Your goal is to be able to accelerate when you want to.

UNDERLINE AND HIGHLIGHT

Motivational speaker and author Zig Ziglar never reads a book or a magazine without a pen in hand. And he never loans one of his underlined books to a friend. "I may buy them one, but I never will let them have mine. It's too valuable." Ziglar has been reading a minimum of three hours a day for 25 years. As a platform speaker, he reads for information, but also for inspiration. "It's not just what I get out of the book that's important," he says, "but what the book gets out of me." Underlining and writing in the margins helps him retain those valuable insights.

Underlining and highlighting can be a useful time tactic. It is a way of making a distinction between the truly important and the unimportant or the merely interesting. You enhance the information value of a book if you underline it and write in it. (Some people use different colors to highlight different kinds of ideas or different topics.) If you're afraid of diminishing the book's value when your heirs sell your estate, use a pencil. The marks can be erased later on.

Underlining choice passages and paragraphs with key information is a great time-saver when you return later to re-enjoy a beautifully crafted sentence, a powerful insight, or an important statistic. Highlighting and underlining is like leaving markers when you're hiking through wilderness. You might find your way back to the campsite without the markers. But the markers surely help.

Highlighting and underlining is an efficient communication technique, too. If you're sending a report or photocopies of correspondence to busy people, highlighting key words and phrases will help them quickly spot the ideas you think are crucial and want to emphasize.

WRITING SHORTCUTS

- *Develop an action plan.* When you're reading or attending a lecture, instead of just taking notes, develop a list of action steps whenever it's appropriate. Action steps are activities that are generated or suggested by the reading material or lecture. Mark with stars those that are most important. The action plan should be separate from your general notes.

- *Note taking.* Create file folders for all the topics you're currently interested in. Whenever you begin a new project, create a new folder, and if you think that it will be a large project, set up folders for each major division. When you come upon useful information or if an idea strikes you, avoid writing about two different ideas on the same card or page. That way, you can quickly insert each new card or sheet in its appropriate folder when you return to your office. Instead of scribbling on envelopes or in the margins of existing material, why not use a full page for the subject (or a set of 3 × 5 cards) at the outset?

- *Make your basic research usable as a first draft whenever possible.* Do the raw research in such a way that it could later be inserted into the manuscript with very little rewriting. Avoid jotting down dates, places, and names in cryptic form. Actually write the draft from the beginning in complete sentences. That way, a step in the process is eliminated and the project is advanced more rapidly toward its final destination.

  Write down enough so that you have something useful to keep and add to, rather than something that is done so poorly that you will have to do everything over from scratch. Avoid needless steps. Make each step as complete as possible.

- *Write succinctly.*   When automobile dealer John Smith attended Harvard Business School, one of his professors required him to write a report every week. There's nothing unusual about writing reports every week in business school. What was different was the length. The reports could be no longer than 500 words. Smith says those assignments were the most difficult exercises he's ever had to do—and the most useful.

  The reports had to be based on cases—long analyses of organizational situations that sometimes ran from 25 to 50 pages. Smith had to boil down his reports that included the most essential ideas into the prescribed 500 words.

  He says those assignments taught him to write in a simple and direct way. Today, Smith owns and runs a big Chevrolet dealership. I asked him what the payoff those reports he wrote years ago had been for his business. He replied: "If you're writing business letters, you'd better write only one page if you expect it to be read by somebody who's busy." He said those writing exercises also taught him to think clearly. The discipline of cutting through a lot of excess to see clearly what the real issues are has served him well outside the classroom.

■ *Abbreviate whenever possible.* If you are in a job that requires you to make notes or keep a journal, it's smart to develop an abbreviation system. Create an index at the beginning of your notes that indicates what the commonly used abbreviations are—the words, names, and expressions that you'll be using. Lawyers do this regularly in long legal documents, stating an abbreviation in parentheses the first time certain names are used and then using that abbreviation throughout the document.

Media consultant Don Anthony uses standard abbreviations when he writes directions. At first that may seem silly—until you think how many times in your life you ask for directions. So, Anthony has learned to write "TL" for turn left; "TR" for turn right; "D" for distance; and "T" for time. If someone invites Anthony to a reception that is 2.4 miles outside the beltway, where he is to turn left at exit 33, go 1.3 miles, and then turn left at King Ave, he will write: "outside beltway 2.4 miles, TL exit 33, go 1.3 miles, TL King Ave." Anthony doesn't abbreviate the names of streets—that can lead to mistakes—but abbreviates virtually everything else. He says this little tactic through the years has saved him a lot of time, and because he has standardized his own abbreviations, he has eliminated errors.

Don Anthony has created his own shorthand system. Some people use standard shorthand. Whatever system you use, make sure your abbreviations make sense. There's really little reason to write out words that you use over and over again, like *with*, *between, the,* and *because,* if you are the only person who'll be using your notes.

If you do much writing, learn the standard abbreviations that editors use. If you have a secretary or assistant, have him or her learn the abbreviations and then use them when you revise your documents and reports. A complete list of these abbreviations can be found in many good dictionaries and reference books.

■ *Use templates.* As a child you used plastic or wooden templates to draw letters and designs. This kindergarten routine can be applied to everyday situations in the adult world.

You can adapt letters of acknowledgment, confirmations, and routine announcements from templates instead of starting them from scratch each time. Previously written material can serve as a guide. You will save a lot of time and increase the quality of your work if you will find examples of your (or somebody else's) best letters, reports, invoices, contracts, and proposals to use as a guide for your efforts.

If you are a meeting planner, prepare a fact sheet that can be sent to the hotel or convention facility. This sheet provides information about your group and specific requirements. Using this sheet, which can be faxed quickly, the meeting planner can save lots of time by not having to answer so many questions on the phone.

With the advent of the computer, it's easier than ever to use templates. All sorts of announcements, letters, newsletters, forms, and reports can be left in a file and customized by your changing only a few words or details. Even long documents like proposals can be used again and again by your adapting them for a particular situation.

Essence magazine editor Susan Taylor has created some 40 basic letters to use as templates. One letter is a response to a request for donations, another is a thank-you letter, one is a rejection letter, one a request for revision. She has what she calls a "warm word" letter that she will tell her secretary to customize for a specific person or group.

The key word with all templates is *customize*. You can always give a template a personalized touch with a handwritten note at the bottom of the form. And with a computer, you can change a few key words or add some new ones that give the message a personal feel.

If you are an officer of an organization that meets regularly, there's usually no need to prepare a separate meeting announcement to send to the other officers each time a meeting is planned. Use a standard form and leave space for changing the date, time, and place. A space also can be left for any new information that must be provided. But the standard form remains the same.

Routing slips are commonly used in many organizations and save a lot of time. The old-fashioned rubber stamp is useful for many routines. Look for more ways to use standard forms, rubber stamps, or form letters for tasks that are repetitive in nature.

Obviously, templates won't always work well. A bit of common sense and experience will tell you to which situations they won't apply. Sympathy notes, some thank-you messages, and congratulatory messages come to mind. Often a handwritten note is required so that the recipient knows that the message is personal.

એ

USE THE PIGGYBACK PRINCIPLE

Don't give the same speech once. —HARVEY MACKAY

Let's say you have to give a speech somewhere. With just a bit of effort you can make that speech work again later on. Some of its components probably can be used in a different setting. You may even be able to use the same basic speech elsewhere, especially if you take the time to edit and polish it. Professional speakers are called upon to make customized presentations all the time, but they will use illustrations, anecdotes, and quotations that have proven successful in previous presentations. They mix old with new.

George Frideric Handel used this tactic when he took material from his earlier works and inserted it into the *Messiah*. Beethoven also borrowed from earlier works to use in his later works. Some critics think they both may have done too much borrowing, but the criticism seems not to have affected the power or the popularity of their work.

There are many other ways to use the piggyback tactic. One is to practice what novelist Danielle Steel calls "geographic economy." She waits until she has several things to do in the same general area of town, instead of setting out for a destination every time she thinks of something. A sales representative with a national travel agency told me that she makes some of her sales calls that way. When she's out on a scheduled sales appointment, she often will make a few "cold calls" in the same locality as the scheduled appointment.

Margaret Barrett, who's a prize-winning professional photographer, wife, and mother, practices geographic economy in her home. She groups tasks geographically, like carrying the trash out when she leaves for a photographic assignment. By advance planning, Barrett avoids making a trip just to take out the trash. She waits to do that until it's time to go to her car. "I try not to go back for anything," Barrett says. "Going back-and-forth is what takes your time."

One workshop participant does what she calls "batching" errands. She creates a batch of errands and then does them all at once. "You often can do in 20 minutes what might otherwise take an hour if done individually," she says. Another participant plans her errands so that when she is in her car, all of her stops are on the right side of the street, starting at the closest point. She then turns around and runs errands on the opposite side of the street. This way, she avoids left turns, waiting for two-way traffic to clear.

ᘓ 5 ᘓ

Find Hidden Time

ᘓ
MAKE THE MOST OF DOWNTIME AND IN-BETWEEN TIME

Making use of your downtime may mean taking a paperback with you to the dentist's or doctor's office. That way you won't have to read their magazines and other cast-offs. A public relations director who attended one of my workshops told the group that he has a stack of reading materials beside his phone that he scans whenever he's put on hold. One salesperson I know who spends lots of time in airports told me, "When I get off the plane, on my way to the baggage area, I stop at a pay phone and make my phone calls. By the time I've finished, my luggage has arrived. If I'm doing something with my time, I'm not wasting it."

Zig Ziglar tries to have something with him to read whenever he has to stand in a line anywhere. Leland Strange, CEO of Intelligent Systems, is so intent on not losing in-between time that he carries technical reports and trade journals along with him in his car. He told me that he's able to read a few lines while he's waiting at stoplights, or when traffic is backed up on the expressway. Anne Sonnee, a workshop participant, does something similar. She keeps a letter opener in her car. She takes a stack of mail with her and glances through the letters at stoplights. Sonnee says that 75 percent of it is junk mail anyway. Her sorting is usually complete by the time she reaches her office, where she throws the junk mail away.

Linda Miles owns her own consulting firm and averages some 130 engagements a year. She spends many days on planes each year, traveling from place to place. Miles believes it's critical to keep in touch with her long list of clients. So, she writes notes to them while she's on planes. "I'm strapped in," she says. "Why not?"

Recently a fellow passenger struck up a conversation with her while they were waiting for their baggage. He said, "I watched you on the plane. For 2 hours and 48 minutes you did nothing but write notes. I'll bet your boss is proud of you." Linda Miles replied, "I am."

Colette O'Brien, who owns a travel agency with many overseas clients, takes a sheaf of fax pads with her on the plane. In flight, she writes out fax messages. When she lands, O'Brien finds a business center, where she sends the messages to her clients. She says the fax message is particularly effective across time zones. The messages will be waiting for her clients when they open their fax machines.

No matter how efficient you may try to be, people will keep you waiting: you'll miss buses, subways, and planes, you'll have unexpected layovers. You may have planned everything as carefully as possible, but there you are in an airport with three unexpected hours to make use of.

Here's what the high achievers do. I've heard it again and again: "I take a book along. I do some writing. I edit a report. I check my voice mail and make my calls. I dictate letters on my machine."

MAKE A GAME OUT OF SAVING TIME

Mark H. McCormack approaches many a situation like it's a game. He tries to think of "quick cuts"—tactics that allow him to reduce time-wasting activities. He knows which restaurants are slow, which are fast, which elevators are the fastest in certain buildings, which airlines are on time, and which handle baggage most efficiently, and which streets and lanes of traffic are fastest.[3]

Here's a tip from Kathy Saunders, who's employed by Corporate Environments of Georgia Inc., a highly successful office equipment company: "When I first arrive at work, I go through my in-box and sort all the items by importance/difficulty. I mentally assign a limited amount of time to each item and then race myself against the set time, trying to finish each task with time left over. Usually, I get more done than I expected."

This is the same approach that an athlete uses. Really fine athletes compete against others, but they also compete against themselves, trying to better their own times and general performance.

There are several benefits that come from treating time tactics as a game.

- You can make mundane tasks fun. Even the most exciting jobs have some mundane, unexciting chores associated with them.

- Competition with yourself may induce what some psychologists call "flow-state" behavior. Flow-state behavior is an altered state of consciousness wherein time seems to be suspended and high levels of effort and accomplishment are attained. (See "Tap into the Power of the 'Flow State'" in Chapter 6.)

- The quality of your work will improve. The goal should be doing it quicker and doing it better. A good hurdler isn't concerned just with running 100 meters at a faster time. The hurdler doesn't want to knock down the hurdles either.

Individuals, small groups, or even entire departments enjoy gamelike activities, such as competing to see how long they can go with zero defects or how many sales their entire unit can make. This induces cooperation as well as excitement.

Milliken & Co. Inc.—a privately owned company that produces textile and chemical products—used this tactic to win the Malcolm Baldrige National Quality Award. Milliken is big on what it calls "scorekeeping"—evaluating what is going on. Milliken believes that scorekeeping is essential for improvement. One of the company's favorite sayings is: "If we aren't keeping score, we are only practicing," Milliken people also believe in letting associates know what the score is. Scoreboards are everywhere in the plants. They are believed to create excitement, enthusiasm, fun, and pride. They provide visual stimulation, new ideas, better communication, a sense of accomplishment, and ownership.

Time tactics is a game that can be played alone or with others. Everyone can win. The real losers are those who don't play.

ॐ

USE YOUR COMMUTE TIME—OR ELIMINATE THE COMMUTE

If you work at the airport, you probably won't want to live at the end of the runway so that you can be close to work. Or if you work at a plant located in the midst of a deteriorating, crime-infested area, you probably won't want to live in the neighborhood.

However, even a commute of 30 minutes one way each day adds up to a staggering total in a few years. If you haven't calculated the total, you probably will be astonished at the results. Thirty minutes a day each way for 50 weeks comes to 250 hours—over 6 weeks of 8-hour days—each year. Six weeks!

If you commute one hour each way—and many people do—you spend over three months of eight-hour days on the road each year. If you earn, say, $50,000 per year, you will have spent $6250 per year in your car for the 30-minute commute and $12,250 for the hour commute—not counting the extra time and money spent for gasoline, tires, and so on. (Look again at the chart in Chapter 1.) It may seem like a great bargain to live way out in the boonies, but it may not be a bargain at all. If you're doing that for economic reasons alone, you should calculate how much the cost is in terms of time and money forgone.

You may choose to live far from work because you like the lifestyle. You may detest congestion, or you may want a change of pace in a different environment every day. But if you want to live optimally, you will want to give serious consideration to trying to find the lifestyle you want nearer your work.

You may commute by bus or train. I admit that I've encountered a number of people who say they love the ride to work. Some of them know the other riders they see each day, and enjoy visiting with them. Others say the ride provides them with an uninterrupted opportunity to read, write, organize their thoughts for a presentation of paper, do dictation, or just be alone with their thoughts. That's if someone else is doing the driving.

Congestion is getting worse, not better, in most metropolitan areas, and many job sites are far from rapid transit. Some companies are creating satellite communication centers in suburban areas so that employees have the option of telecommuting. In a satellite office, fellow workers can still enjoy face-to-face contact within the context of the company culture. They may not use the satellite office every day, but it is an option to a long commute to their regular office. Jack M. Niles, a consultant who coined the term *telecommuting,* estimates that 3 million workers in the United States practice it regularly, most of them one or two days a week. Niles feels that the number will grow to about 11 million by the year 2000—and even more if there is another oil crisis.

If you have to drive on a long commute each day, this time need not be totally wasted. It's a good time to be alone with your thoughts. You can do planning with minimum interruptions. You can use a car phone to make calls. If you have an advanced voice mail system, you can do dictation. And, of course, you can use a compact dictating unit in the car. You can also listen to educational and motivational tapes.

But for most commuters most of the time, the long drive is a wasteful and sometimes stressful experience. Give serious thought to eliminating it or making it work for you.

❧
CREATE CHUNKS OF TIME

Years ago management guru Peter Drucker began to urge managers to organize their work so that they have "blocks" or "chunks" of time. These chunks are intervals when managers are not interrupted, when they can focus on their work. The alternative to creating chunks is *churning*—like a computer spending so much time going back and forth from one program to another that very little is accomplished in any one of them.

Following Drucker's advice is not easy. Interruptions are a way of life for many people. In some occupations, workers are continuously bombarded by phone calls and personal intrusions. It's one long blur of interactions.

The producer of live telecasts or the manager of a busy restaurant will have to make hundreds of decisions during the course of a few hours. Yet, even these professionals can create a chunk of time before air time, or before customers begin to arrive, if they are creative and disciplined.

Here are some suggestions for creating chunks of time:

- *Come early or leave late.* Many top people come early to the office because they know the phone won't start ringing or other people won't be there. This is the tactic used by Kay Koplovitz, CEO of USA Network. Or they work late when they know the nine-to-five employees are gone and the phone stops ringing. (If you're trying to achieve balance in your life, avoid coming early *and* staying late except for short periods of time.)

- *Stay away from work.* Some people who are very successful will stay at home one day a week or perhaps two half-days a week. This way, they create chunks of time. Obviously, you will need to have an employer that permits this option, or you will have to be self-employed.

- *Create chunks in-between.* Dr. W. Dallas Hall, who's director of the Clinical Research Center at Emory University School of Medicine, finds his chunks of time traveling between his three offices. One is at the main campus, one is at Grady Hospital, and one is in the nearby town of Decatur. "At first I thought it would be really time-inefficient to have three offices. I have been pleasantly surprised. I find I get more work done in three places than in one."

  Hall says having another office to go to gives him with a wonderful escape hatch: "The 15 minutes I spend driving from one office to the other provides me some of the most wonderful time in the day for thinking, for collecting my thoughts."

  Many frequent fliers find their chunks of time on the plane. "I love my plane time," *Essence* editor Susan Taylor told me. "It's a great time to get my work done." As we have already seen, commute time, which for most people is an almost complete loss, can be transformed into a valuable chunk of time.

■ *Create chunks of time for crucial one-on-one meetings.*   If an appointment is very important, tell your assistant or secretary that you don't want any interruptions except for emergencies or interruptions that have a clearly spelled out priority.

John Olsen, president of the Fairview Foundation and a former chairman of the National Association of Hospital Developers, has used this tactic for years. He calls such meetings with his people "time-certain appointments." Olsen described the way he manages them: "I have one of my staff members visiting with me this morning around 10 and we both want to create what we call time-certain hours in which that time is his and he has 30 to 45 minutes, depending on what the push is."

The "time-certain appointment" tells the staff member that he or she is so important that nothing else will happen in that block of time. No phone calls. No interruptions. It also provides an opportunity to do something in depth.

What about the phone calls that come in during that time? Olsen deals with them in chunks of time, too. He will take a phone call at any time if he's not in a time-certain appointment or doing something else that precludes interruptions. But he follows a routine of doing call-backs during two blocks of time, one in the morning and the other toward the end of the day. Olsen sums it up: "I try to create for myself uninterrupted blocks of time, and I try to work in blocks of two and three hours."

BE A CONTRARIAN

Read every day something no one else is reading.
Think every day something no one else is thinking.
It is bad for the mind to be always part of unanimity.
                                        —CHRISTOPHER MORLEY

What is a contrarian? On Wall Street, a contrarian is someone who buys when most people are selling and sells when most people are buying. If everyone else is marking time, the contrarian is buying or selling like crazy.

There are many ways to use contrarian principles in everyday life. During the 1980s, Ken Cooper wrote a book on the subject with the intriguing title, *Always Bear Left.* Cooper's comprehensive recommendation? Live "off peak" in order to avoid the rush.[4]

Applying contrarian principles to time management means that you do all sorts of things when nobody else is doing them. A contrarian cashes checks and shops when other people are not forming long lines. You don't try to cash a check on Friday afternoon. You don't buy your groceries on Friday afternoon either. You go to a 24-hour grocery store at 11 p.m. or perhaps at 6 a.m.

Contrarians check out of their hotel when other people aren't, or they use the hotel's automatic checkout. It's silly to stand in a long checkout line at midmorning if you can do it before the crowd arrives. At the office, they use the computer printer or the photocopier during lunch—when most employees are gone.

Contrarians won't even think about buying presents during the holiday season. I certainly don't. I buy my presents when I see them, even if I don't know who might eventually receive them. If it's something that I really love and believe that someone someday will love it too, I buy it. Then I put it in a big trunk, which my daughters have always called the "treasure chest." When there's a birthday or holiday, I visit the treasure chest and usually can find something lovely that can be given as a present. I don't have to stop what I'm doing to go out to buy something that I may not like very much, and probably will pay top dollar for, just because it's somebody's birthday or because it's the holiday season.

Unfortunately, I don't know who to thank for this tactic. Perhaps I thought it up myself, but it has been a great success in my family for three decades.

Recently, I discovered that Naomi Rhode, the president of the National Speakers Association, uses the same principle, but she does it on a larger and more sophisticated scale than my simple treasure chest. She has a *gift closet,* which she fills with presents from her travels all over the world. She has catalogued all these gifts on her computer, grouped under topics.

Not long ago, she and her husband Jim were houseguests of long-time friends. Afterwards, when they wanted to send them a special gift, Rhode called her personal assistant and told her to select one of 10 black Russian lacquer boxes she had recently purchased abroad—along with a greeting card that she had also selected long in advance. The entire transaction was completed within minutes.

Contrarians make it a point to dine out before the crowds arrive. They avoid restaurants that don't take reservations or that don't honor reservations efficiently. They will go to lunch or dinner early, when the restaurant is less crowded, when the waiters and chefs are less tired, and when the choice of food in the kitchen is best and freshest. Contrarians even save money with this tactic, because some restaurants offer a special price for early diners.

Contrarians try to schedule airline flights for nonpeak hours of the day. That way they avoid wasting time while their plane waits in a line on the runway or in holding patterns when landing. One workshop participant told me that his travel agent has a 24-hour ticketing service. He has found that he gets really prompt service by making his travel reservations late at night, usually after midnight.

Contrarians try to drive during nonpeak hours, too. If everyone else is coming to the office between 7:30 and 9:00, they may want to arrive at 7:00. They zip right in. Or they arrive later and leave later, with many of the same advantages early arrivers enjoy. One workshop participant told me that when he's driving on a trip, he likes to travel late at night or early in the morning. "That's what truck drivers do when they can," he explained. "They do it because there is no traffic then."

Contrarians love the idea of flextime. Many companies and agencies stagger the hours employees work so that the offices are actually open for a longer period of time, but no one person is there during the entire period. The hours overlap. It's great for the organization and it's great for the individuals. A workshop participant wrote: "I come in 30 to 60 minutes before everyone and take no calls for the first hour. I go through my list and find one [task] that that I can accomplish and do it before the phone rings and the crises begin." Flextime is what a contrarian would invent if it didn't already exist.

ૐ

THE FIVE O'CLOCK CLUB

I would rather sleep only five hours and wake up at 5:00 or 5:30 and be in control of my time than to sleep later and spend the entire day controlled by time instead of controlling it.
—DAN BOUCHARD, FORMER BIG-LEAGUE HOCKEY STAR

Mary Kay was the first person to tell me about what she called the "Five O'clock Club." Her reference to this club was an aside to her comments on how the women in her organization managed to get their work done.

Many of the sales associates in Mary Kay's company are women with children. Their daily routine involves cooking breakfast, preparing lunches, and getting the children off to school.

How do they get their sales work done if those chores face them Monday through Friday? Mary Kay answers, "The five o'clock club. Start the day at five o'clock in the morning."

Rising before the sun does, day after day, requires a lot of discipline. But there are many advantages. There are no interruptions. It's quiet and peaceful. You have a great sense of well-being. You feel you are working hard to achieve your goals and whatever good things happen to you, you will deserve them. Mary Kay recommends that her sales associates use this quiet, uninterrupted time to check inventory, make out orders, write thank-you notes, and plan the rest of the day.

I've met many other highly successful people who are members of the five o'clock club, even though they haven't heard about Mary Kay's version of it. They use the early morning hours to jog, to exercise, to write, to meditate, to plan. For many, it's their quiet time, the time they spend reflecting, getting their motor turned on. National Life of Vermont president John H. Harding does some of his best thinking during his early morning workout.

One of the earliest interviews I did with high-profile people was with former U.S. Senator Herman Talmadge, who was at that time one of the nation's most powerful and best-known senators. His press secretary told me to call the Senator anytime after 5. I asked him if he meant morning or afternoon. He told me, "In the morning. The Senator begins work very early."

I wasn't brave enough to call at 5, but I did call at 7 the next morning. Sure enough, Talmadge answered the phone himself, bright and cheerful. I apologized for the early call, but he told me he'd been up for hours. He explained that he started doing it when he was in law school. He learned if he was the first person to get to the library, he could always obtain the reserve books he needed before the other students arrived.

A salesperson who attended one of my seminars wrote about these benefits from getting to her office at seven in the morning: "I'm there two hours before the rest of the group arrives. I can use the copier and fax without waiting in line. I can make phone calls to customer service reps at the factories. And I have time to revise my to-do list that I made out about 3 p.m. the previous afternoon. Then I leave an hour or so before the rest of the group leaves."

USE THE POWER OF LEVERAGE: LEARN TO THINK LAZY

Many of our most important inventions were produced by people who were looking for an easier way to do something. Thomas Edison was fired from an early job as a telegraph operator when it was discovered that he had created a device to let him take short naps on the job. Henry Ford, while still a boy, designed a device that allowed him to shut the gate without having to get out of the wagon. Years later, after he had become a world-famous manufacturer, Ford was still creating devices that made work easier. Ford implemented a feeder line to the factory so that workers wouldn't have to waste their energy walking to get parts. After the feeder line became a standard part of the car-building process, Ford realized that workers' stooping over the assembly line increased fatigue and led to sloppy work and accidents. So, Ford insisted that the entire line be raised by 8 inches. This simple adjustment, which made work less tiring, led to a major increase in productivity.

In the most primitive societies, the only source of energy is the human organism itself. The amount of power that an average adult can generate is less than $\frac{1}{10}$ of 1 horsepower. Obviously, societies that rely on human power alone never get very far. And you as an individual won't get very far either if you rely on physical labor alone.

Sometimes you will hear people complain that life hasn't been fair to those who worked hard all their life and died poor. Life isn't fair or unfair. It simply favors societies and individuals who learn how to exploit energy efficiently.

Ask yourself, "Is there an easier way to do this?" Looking for the easy way out can be the smartest thing you do. Don't confuse busyness with efficiency. An organization's best people sometimes spend their most productive time seemingly daydreaming.

Busyness may, in fact, be counterproductive. "It is necessary to be slightly underemployed if you are to do something significant," says James D. Watson.[5] He is a Nobel laureate who shared the prize with Francis Crick for successfully discovering the genetic code of DNA. The story of how underemployed they were—the stories of their meanderings and long weekends, parties, visits, and other diversions—is told delightfully in *The Double Helix*, a human-side-of-science classic. Watson and Crick had the luxury of being able to study all sorts of ideas, interact with scientists in many fields, attend conferences all over the world. But most of all, Watson and Crick had time to think about what they were reading and hearing and seeing. That's what Watson means when he praises underemployment.

If these two researchers had not received generous research grants, if they had needed to hold down two jobs in order to make ends meet, they probably would not have made the discovery that revolutionized biological research. Thanks to generous support plus the British university tradition that emphasizes contemplation, Watson and Crick were sufficiently underemployed to do something significant.

People on treadmills don't get very far. If you're so busy working that you have no time to think about what you're working at, you'll be unable to make full use of your accomplishments.

Underemployment provides the time between activities to reflect on what you've just finished and think, "What does this mean?" "How can I exploit what I have done?" Underemployment provides the time to figure out other ways than the obvious to use what you're producing. And it provides time to consider how what you've done fits with what's already been done. You can take inventory. There may be resources that lie unused in the filing cabinet storage room that can now be put to use.

When you're underemployed, you have time available to research widely, not narrowly. If you're so absorbed in your own little field, you may not know that something is happening in another area that could have tremendous consequences for what you are doing. Innovations aren't likely to occur unless people have the time to range widely and learn what others are doing.

Only rarely is there a discovery of something totally new. An innovation almost always involves putting two or more known ideas together in a new or novel way. For example, Robert Fulton's commercially successful steamship combined two lines of discoveries. One was the steam engine itself. The other was ship technology. But Fulton had to know a bit about both technologies in order to develop a new one that melded the two. And he needed time to think about them.

Sometimes underemployment is not chosen. Rather it is imposed by an environment that affords limited opportunities, such as India did to young Winston Churchill, who was posted there and matured intellectually when he had large chunks of time available to him. He chose to use those times to begin to read the books he had neglected in college.

Robert J. Broadwater, who led the teams that introduced Coca-Cola to Japan and Fanta to the former Soviet Union, matured intellectually when he was confined in a prison camp in Japan for almost four years during World War II. The commander of the prison, who had taught English in Japan before the war, brought some of the books from his personal library to the camp for the prisoners to read. "That's how I got my liberal arts education," Broadwater told me. "What I learned there became the basis for all the decisions I later made at Coca-Cola."

Something similar happened to performer Julio Iglesias, who did not begin his career as a musician. Music was the result of an accident. Iglesias had studied law and later became a goalie for a soccer team in Madrid. In 1963, he was involved in an auto accident that almost took his life and left him paralyzed for a year. During his recuperation, a nurse gave Julio a guitar, and he began writing songs. Five years later, he won a prestigious Spanish song festival award with a song he wrote entitled "La Vida Sigue Igual" ("Life Goes on Just the Same"). The song became Spain's number-one hit in a matter of days. By 1983, he had sold so many records worldwide that he received a diamond disc from the *Guinness Book of Records*—for selling 100 million records in six languages. Today, his concerts in Madrid draw more people than Madrid's soccer team. Underemployment, plus access to a guitar, set a new career in motion.

Conducter Maxim Shostakovich told me that a reporter once asked his father, Dimitri Shostakovich, how he was able to write so rapidly. The famous composer replied: "I think about it for a long time."

❧ 6 ❧

Learn to Focus

❧
DON'T SCATTER YOUR FORCE

When *Success* magazine celebrated its one-hundredth birthday in 1991, the editors produced some vintage material from earlier issues. One of the most impressive was an excerpt from the February 1898 issue. Author Theodore Dreiser camped outside the laboratory of Thomas A. Edison for three weeks before he could obtain an interview with the famous inventor. Here is part of that interview:

> DREISER: What's the first requisite for success?
>
> EDISON: The ability to apply your physical and mental energies to one problem incessantly without growing weary....You do something all day long, don't you? Everyone does. If you get up at 7 a.m. and go to bed at 11 p.m., you have put in 16 good hours, and it is certain with most men that they have been doing something all the time. The only trouble is that they do it about a great many things, and I do it about one. If they took the time in question and applied it in one direction, to one object, they would succeed.[6]

❧
LEARN TO LISTEN

Most of us spend about 70 to 80 percent of our lives engaged in some form of communication: writing, speaking, or listening. At one time or another, many of us have taken courses designed to teach us how to write, how to read, and how to speak. Such courses can be found in high schools, colleges, and universities.

Yet virtually no formal training in *listening* is available in schools, industry, or business. Listening is without doubt the most important skill in the communication process. A person who has learned how to listen is the one who is most likely to get things right, please the manager, win friends, and recognize opportunities that other people miss.

Listening worked for the legendary John D. Rockefeller. "It has been our policy to hear patiently and discuss frankly until the last shred of evidence is on the table before trying to reach a conclusion," John D. Rockefeller once stated. Rockefeller was known to be deliberate and often seemingly slow in arriving at a decision. He refused to be rushed into making a decision. His motto was, "Let the other fellow talk."[7]

If you practice just a little bit at golf, you may see some difference in your golf score. But only a small amount of practice at listening can produce dramatic results.

If you listen when your manager asks you to do something, you increase the chances that you'll do it right and not have to do it over. If you listen when somebody gives you directions, you're less likely to get lost. If you listen to what your customers really want, you can avoid wasting time and money on what they don't want and won't buy.

Here are a few important listening rules:

- *Recognize that listening is an active process, not a passive one.* Be as mentally alert as a shortstop pouncing on a hard-hit grounder.

- *Don't talk too much yourself.* It's difficult to talk and listen at the same time. Multimillionaire J. B. Fuqua has an earned reputation for saying little and listening much. He has been known to sit through major business meetings without making a single comment. He told me once, "There's a reason why God gave us two ears and one mouth. We should listen more than we talk."

    In order to avoid talking too much and losing sales, some trainers recommend using the burning match approach. Pretend that you're holding a burning match in your hand. As soon as you think the flame is getting too close to your fingers, stop talking and seek some feedback from the other person.

- *Don't look too good or talk too wise.* The people you talk to may be self-conscious or shy. They may become defensive because they don't want to sound inarticulate. Even if you're an expert on a topic, learn to keep quiet sometimes and show that you want to know more than you already do.

- *Be interested and show it.* There's nothing more flattering to someone than to be genuinely interested in them. Mary Kay told me that she imagines that every person she meets has a sign around their neck that says, "Make Me Feel Important."

  Beware of telling other people how they feel. But you can ask, "How do *you* feel about that?"

- *Concentrate.* Don't let your mind wander. You can develop your concentration powers through practice at shutting out distractions.

- *Don't jump to conclusions.* Hear the other person out. You should respond only after you're sure you have a complete picture of the other person's point of view. Just because they've paused doesn't mean they've finished saying everything they want to say.

- *Don't spend all your time thinking about what your next response or brilliant remark will be.* After almost three decades of university teaching, I've observed that the students who talk the most in class often aren't the ones who make the highest grades. My guess is that the constant talkers aren't listening to the instructor or to other students, but are devoting most of their time thinking about what to say next.

- *Motivate people to tell you more.* Just a small application of reinforcement theory will work wonders. Sometimes in the early part of a conversation or interview, there will be a fluff and useless chatter. Then will come a fine insight, a quotable statement, or a valuable piece of information. When this happens, reward the other person with a statement of honest appreciation, like "That's a great story," or "What a terrific idea."

You get the kind of behavior that you reinforce. So, wait until someone does something that you like and reward it. You can stimulate a lot of useful and entertaining conversation just by giving good feedback.

- *Listen for ideas, not just words.* Try to paint a mental picture of what you hear.

- *Listen discriminatingly.* Concentrate on key facts and try to ignore trivia and fluff.

- *Let the other person know you're listening.* One way is to maintain eye contact. Listen with your eyes as well as your ears. Another way is to use interjections. An occasional "Yes," "I see," or "Is that so?" shows the other person that you're still there, that you're still interested. In Japan, when two Japanese converse, they use reply words called *aizuchi*. The word *aizuchi* comes from the word *ai*, which means "doing something together," and the word *zuchi*, which refers to a hammer. Two Japanese talking together, frequently exchanging reply words, sound like two swordsmiths hammering on a blade. In our culture, you won't need to take it that far, but an occasional reply word or a nodding of the head won't hurt.

- *Use the silent pause.* If you have been using reply words, interjections, and nods throughout the conversation, occasionally stop responding in order to tease out valuable information. It's a device that journalists use all the time. Many individuals cannot deal with silence or a lack of response, and they will rush in to fill the silence with a comment.

- *Turn off your own worries.* If you are emotionally distracted, you may throw up a screen through which information will not readily penetrate.

- *React to ideas, not to the person.* The other individual may have mannerisms that irritate you, but train yourself to listen to what is being said. Even a bitter enemy will say truths that need to be heard.

- *Watch for nonverbal cues.* The other party may be speaking words that are discrepant from what is actually being said nonverbally. Learn to read people and situations.

- *Read between the lines.*   Pay attention to what isn't said, information or ideas that aren't discussed, questions that aren't answered fully.

- *Record what you hear.*   Getting out a pen and paper or a tape recorder may be counterproductive in certain situations. But later on, making notes that capture essential facts and important ideas may prove to be very valuable. If you do use a tape recorder, request permission to use it and then try to place it outside the direct vision of the interviewee. Many people become very self-conscious if a microphone or a tape recorder is placed directly in front of them. Even though they may not object to being recorded, their remarks become overly guarded.

- *Get and give feedback.*   One of the best ways is to recapitulate what has just been said. You can comment, "Just to make sure that I understand what it is you want me to do, here's the way I understand it...."

- *Make applications of what is heard.*   People in sales, especially, should listen to prospects' and customers' comments and use them to help close the sale.

🙵
SPEND MORE TIME IN THE NOW

Most people are just slightly ahead of the time or slightly behind. They are never precisely in the moment, in the now. If they are engaged in conversation with someone, they may be thinking about what they just said or what the other person just said or they may be thinking about what they will say next. Or they may even be thinking about something entirely different.

We can learn a valuable lesson from the craft of acting. The finest actors are in the now. They listen so intently that even though they may have memorized their lines perfectly, there is a sense in which what they say next will be something new. Two actors doing a scene really "act" only one line: the first line. After that, every additional line that is said is a reaction to what the other actor has just said or done.

Like accomplished actors, we can learn to be in the now. Being in the "now" involves focus. Focus has two elements. One is targeting. We pay attention to what is happening. The other is intensity. Because we concentrate all of our power on a single event in real time, there is intensity.

I asked Gunther Gebel-Williams, the celebrated circus performer, what advice he had given his son, who's following his father's career as an animal trainer.

"I told him to be there," Gebel-Williams replied.

I was not sure exactly what he meant. Perhaps it was a father telling his son to always show up for work —the way he had for over 10,000 straight performances. But he had something else in mind.

"When he's in the ring with lions, tigers, and leopards, he can't be somewhere else. He must never let his mind wander," the best-known animal trainer in the world explained. "He must be in the ring mentally."

It's pretty obvious how dangerous it is to let your mind wander in a circus ring when you're surrounded by dangerous animals. But letting your mind wander can be disastrous to virtually any career.

Auto-leasing expert Dick Biggs remembers a humiliating lapse of attention that he can laugh about now, but which at the time was anything but funny. It was at the start of the Second Annual Chattahoochee Road Runners 10-kilometer race in Atlanta. The sponsor that year was Coca-Cola. As a part of the promotion, Diet Coke was prominently displayed on race applications and emphasized in the media outlets. The Diet Coke logo was displayed on the T-shirts and race numbers.

On race morning, Dick Biggs, who was honorary president of the event, stood on the platform, and stated: "We're delighted with such a large turnout and especially grateful to our sponsor...Diet Pepsi." The Coca-Cola representative, who was standing directly behind Biggs, hissed: "It's Diet Coke, you idiot! (Actually, he used a different word than *idiot*.) Over 1200 runners howled. And Biggs was humiliated, mortified. "I knew the facts, but I was out of focus," Biggs says. "On that fateful day, I learned that focus is more important than facts."

TAP INTO THE POWER OF THE "FLOW STATE"

University of Chicago psychologist Mihaly Csikszentmihalyi studies "flow-state" behavior. Flow-state behavior is activity that occurs during periods of deep concentration and results in a mental state so focused that irrelevant tasks are ignored. Athletes sometimes use the expression "playing in your zone" to describe those times when they are performing well above their abilities, when everything is clicking.

Csikszentmihalyi has had some success inducing flow-state behavior through the challenge of gamelike situations. He says that a flow state is most likely to occur when individuals are in situations in which their ability is about equal to the difficulty of their tasks. If the task is too difficult, individuals feel anxious. If the task is not difficult enough, they get bored.

After I had mentioned flow-state behavior before a large audience, Paul Ottinger, who is a master carpenter from Pennsylvania, told me his experience. Several years ago he entered a local carpentry competition in Philadelphia that was sponsored by the International Brotherhood of Carpenters. For hours he worked on his project, concentrating on nothing but the job. "It was just me and my tools," Ottinger recalled. After he had finished the project that subsequently took first prize, he noticed that a crowd of people had gathered around him. Ottinger hadn't even noticed they were there.

The reason flow-state behavior is listed as a time tactic is because people who experience it report a loss of awareness of time. They also produce an enormous amount of high-level work during the flow-state episode. Betty Edwards' book *Drawing on the Right Side of the Brain* describes techniques that can lead to experiences that are similar, if not the same as, flow-state behavior. Edwards' approach is based on the idea that the left mode of the brain (L) is verbal, analytic, symbolic, rational, digital, logical, and linear. The right mode of the brain (R) is nonverbal, synthetic, nonrational, intuitive, and holistic.

Edwards' book includes a number of exercises to help readers gain experience doing the "L-R shift." Here's how Edwards describes the experience: "When I'm really working well, it's like nothing else I've ever experienced. I feel at one with the work: the painter, the painting, it's all one. I feel excited, but calm—exhilarated, but in full control. It's not exactly happiness; it's more like bliss."[8]

PASSION AND OBSESSION

This time tactic isn't for everyone. You may be an achiever but have no interest in obsessions. I understand perfectly. Some of the people I've interviewed have paid a price for their success that most people would not want to pay. But there is no denying that people who become obsessed by a task or a career or a cause get a lot done, and they often do it efficiently.

Erskine Caldwell, author of *Tobacco Road* and *God's Little Acre,* comes to mind. He told me that three marriages had come apart and he did not have many close friends because he always put his work ahead of everything else.

Looking back over five decades of phenomenal financial successes, J. B. Fuqua told me that his one big regret was that he had developed no interests outside his business. Author Isaac Asimov told me that he didn't want to take vacations because that would mean interrupting his writing. Asimov spent hour upon hour seated in front of his typewriter grinding out book after book. For a number of years, he produced a book a month. When I asked what he worked at hardest, he answered, "Being pleasant when somebody interrupts my writing."

Henry Ford once stated, "I had plenty of time, for I never left my business. I do not believe a man can ever leave his business. He ought to think of it by day and dream of it by night."[9]

People who are dismayed at the amount of time and energy such individuals devote to their obsessions sometimes forget that they may not regard this as sacrifice but as pleasure. Lee Trevino says, "I just love the game."

Perhaps, then, we should not feel sorry for obsessed people. Obsessions come in all shapes and sizes. Some are based upon guilt, others on ignorance, gullibility, or frustration. But some obsessions, like Trevino's, are based on love of what they do, and the obsession enriches everything they touch.

7

Pace Yourself

CREATE ROUTINES: DISCOVER YOUR WORK RHYTHMS

The word *Methodist* is associated with the names of John Wesley and Charles Wesley, who were theological students at Oxford University in the eighteenth century. The Wesley brothers and a few fellow students formed a small group that they called the "Holy Club." The club had strict rules about when and how often they would pray, read Scripture, give alms to the poor, and the like. They in effect developed a routine or *method* for religious activities. Members of the club were quickly nicknamed "methodists" by their classmates. That word eventually became attached to the religious denomination that the Wesleys founded.

The Wesleys were tapping an ancient idea found in many religions. The ancient Hebrews followed a very specific calendar. So did many old Catholic orders of monks and nuns, and some still do. Mohammed made routines a key element in the religion he founded. Muslims today pray five times daily, beginning at the very first light of day and reserve one month of the year, Ramadan, for fasting and abstinence.

Mozart was portrayed in *Amadeus* as a harum-scarum, capricious genius. Yet from the time that Mozart was 15 years old until his death, his output was so constant that it could be boiled down to an algebraic equation.

Among the people I know, historian Mel Kranzberg writes 10 letters every morning that he's in his office. Joe Charbonneau, a leading professional speaker, requires his telemarketing people to make 13 telephone contacts on Monday, 13 on Tuesday, 12 on Wednesday, and 12 on Thursday. Friday is spent calling back people who were missed during the week.

Many writers create a routine for working every day between certain hours, and producing a required number of words before they stop. This approach works for me. If I get into the habit of writing about 1000 words a day, and if I do that for a few days, those thousand words will come readily. Then I can push the number up a bit to perhaps 1200 words or even several thousand words after a few days. It's uncanny how the mind can supply a quota of words every day if you get into the routine of requiring the mind to do it.

I am not sure why this happens. Perhaps the unconscious mind is getting ready for a regular command. Perhaps the body has a strong proclivity toward patterns or regular rhythms and habits. Perhaps it is tied to the internal body clock that all of us have. But I do know that innumerable high achievers have learned to use these patterns, rhythms, and habits like surfers riding waves.

Chronobiologists have found that the biggest waves come at certain times of the day. For most people, the big waves tend to start arriving around 11 a.m, although some early risers report big ones around daybreak or even in the middle of the night. The high-wave phase that starts around 11 a.m. usually lasts about two hours and then subsides, whether we eat lunch or not. (It is unfortunate that the peak creative time for many individuals is in the middle of the day, when most people stop what they are doing to to go somewhere to eat.) Another high-wave phase begins about 4 p.m. and lasts until about 6 p.m., again when many people are driving home.

This chronobiological pattern doesn't fit everyone. So you will need to experiment to see what times work best for any routine that you are thinking about establishing. You may want to try to do noncreative tasks, like opening letters, filing, or reading the paper, in the early morning. Do the most mentally demanding work between 11 a.m. and 1 p.m. and from 4 p.m. to 6 p.m. Get to know your own body. Learn to recognize when your peak performance times occur and use them to accomplish your most demanding tasks during those times.

Your aim should be to turn productive activity into routines and habits as often as possible. Routines mean that your unconscious mind knows in advance what is going to be required. It can start getting ready for the command while you're doing something else. Established routines have sociological benefits too. Others around you learn your habits and can adjust to them.

ॐ

ADAPT TO THE RHYTHMS AROUND YOU

Every human organization, large and small, has rhythms and goes through cycles. There is a time to buy, a time to sell, a time to do the books. Sometimes a society will resist change for decades. Then, almost abruptly a revolution will occur. A person who might have been hanged one year will be chosen president the next. That very thing happened in recent years in Eastern Europe. Activities that had once been treasonable offenses became the order of the day.

Recognizing and adapting to rhythms and cycles is essential to success. You might have the greatest advertising concept in the world, but if you present it at a time when companies have completed their advertising budgets, you're out of luck. It probably won't be seriously considered until months later.

Publishers' representatives who call on college campuses know that certain months are better than others to get professors to consider new textbooks. If they visit at other times, the decisions will have been made and the orders placed.

This tactic does not preclude relationship-building visits at other times. Those kinds of visits often can be critical. If you're in sales, and you come by to visit when you know the customer isn't buying and he knows you know, that kind of visit may pay off down the road. But the reason it pays off is because you know the cycle and have adapted to it.

Make it your business to know your customer's business. Learn the rhythms and cycles of the business you deal with. "If you mind just your own business, you may soon be out of business," says management consultant Austin McGonigle.

Many organizational cycles are organized around days and hours, not just months and seasons. If you're in public relations, don't call a daily newspaper with a story idea at four o'clock in the afternoon. Why? Because four o'clock is probably the deadline for a morning paper. Television has its deadlines, too, for stories for the morning and evening news (except for breaking stories).

Every magazine has a deadline day. Magazines and newspapers schedule editors' meetings on certain days and hours of the week. Television stations and networks do the same. If you call during that meeting, most of the decision makers won't be able to talk to you.

It's not always easy to know what's happening in somebody else's business. But with hard work, research, and a bit of luck, you sometimes can catch the situation at just the right time. When that happens, it's almost magical to see things fall into place.

Minding your customer's business can be a systematic undertaking. Create a file for each of your customers and fill it with clippings and informative articles. Read your customer's trade publications. By becoming knowledgeable, you'll be able to anticipate the peaks and valleys of the industry, and how better to respond to high-demand periods.

For example, if you're in the temporary-service business and some of your clients are accounting firms, you know what will happen on April 15. So consider making a call in January when you say something like: "We know you're going to be going crazy in a few weeks. Will you need some temporary people? If you do, we are here to help you."

In other fields, the demand cycle may not be as obvious as that of an accounting firm. One financial adviser I know works with a number of physicians. After she establishes a relationship, she finds out what day of week and time of day are best for calls, and she puts that in her Rolodex.

Experienced travelers know that the rhythms are different from country to country and often between regions in the same country. In the Caribbean, they operate on what is called "island time." It's a blend of *manana* and "Take it easy, mon." In that region, you are wasting time and effort if you try to force islanders to run on American time. If you insist on speeding up things, all you will get for your efforts will be resistance, sullen stares, and perhaps deliberate delays and sabotage. On the islands, and elsewhere in the world, when the rhythm is slower than your own, and you have no power to change it, effective time tacticians adapt to that rhythm and learn to use the downtime effectively.

Individuals operate on different rhythms too. Last winter, I was standing in line at a pastry shop. The saleswoman was waiting on a customer in front of me. She shouldn't mind, I thought, if I ask how much my selection will cost, and leave the exact change on the counter.

But she ignored me. I asked the question again, but there was no response. She continued wrapping the other customer's package, and counted out his change. I was slightly annoyed, but did my best to disguise it. When the customer had been fully taken care of, she turned her attention to me.

Looking at the package of pastries that I had selected, she said, "I think we have some fresher ones here." She picked up my package and exchanged it for another. Then she asked: "Would you like for me to heat them up for you?" I hadn't even known that this service was available. I nodded and she popped them into the oven.

Three or four minutes later I had some tasty, warm pastries, and headed to my appointment. By adapting to her rhythm, I was able to get more than I had expected. Learning to adjust good-naturedly to the prevailing rhythm of the social situation is not only wise and pleasant but can be unexpectedly rewarding too.

"I don't mean to be impolite, but don't put a slow-talking Southerner on the phone to pitch stories to New York editors and writers," a top editor told a group of public relations executives. She explained that editors and writers in the big leagues have so many people wanting them to do stories that they must make decisions very quickly about how much they can afford to listen to. Admittedly, they make mistakes by judging too hastily. But if someone wants to do business in that league, they have to learn to talk fast and get to the point quickly. They have to adapt to the gatekeeper's rhythm.

Abraham Lincoln clearly understood the rhythms of communication. Lincoln once described to a friend how he told an anecdote: "If you have an auditor who has the time and is inclined to listen, lengthen it out slowly as if from a jug. If you have a poor listener, hasten it, shorten it, and shoot it out of a pop gun."[10]

In order to make social and individuals' rhythms work for you instead of against you, two traits are required. One is the ability to observe carefully. You won't adapt successfully unless you can figure out what the rhythm is. The other is the willingness to learn and adapt. People who always insist on having their own way and their own rhythm are bound to take some pounding.

MASTER YOUR MOODS

You may not be able to control the situation, but you can always control your reaction. —AUSTIN MCGONIGLE

Depression and bad moods are notorious thieves of time. In a depression or bad mood, many people stop doing anything productive and often do things that are destructive.

Even the most up-beat individuals must occasionally confront a wily time thief called depression. If you can learn how to fight off bad moods and keep them from making off with your day, you will have acquired an invaluable ability. Here's how:

- *Develop your willpower through exercise.* The ability to keep going when it's hard to keep going is the mark of a true pro. Ray Charles, the singer, once described how much he enjoyed performing before a crowd, how there was nothing like the exhilaration of being in front of a big crowd when it's with you. I asked: "And what do you do when the crowd is small and isn't with you?" Ray Charles replied: "That's when you find out whether you're a pro or not. That's when you work harder than ever."

When Mark Twain was completing his book on the Mississippi River, he finished it through sheer willpower. Here's what he wrote to a friend:

The weather turned cold, and we had to rush home, while I still lacked thirty thousand words. I had been sick and got delayed. I am going to write all day and two-thirds of the night until the thing is done or break down at it. The spur and burden of the contract are intolerable to me....I went to work at nine o'clock yesterday morning and went to bed an hour after midnight. Result of the day (mainly stolen from books though credit given), 9500 words, so I reduced my burden by one-third in one day....I have nothing more to borrow or steal; the rest must all be written. It is ten day's work, and unless something breaks it will be finished in five.[11]

Doing a task through sheer discipline creates muscles that get stronger every time you use them. This is what joggers do when their legs are worn out and ready to collapse. This is what swimmers do when their lungs are burning and their arms feel heavy as lead.

A scuba-diving instructor once told me: "It's amazing how far you can swim underwater when you think you're out of air. You think you have no more air left; but, through willpower, you can keep on swimming." By the time the course was over, I had discovered that what he told me was true. I could swim longer than I thought I could, even when I thought I had no air left.

■ *Use affirmation therapy.* If you are feeling depressed or suffering from a case of the blahs, you may be able to get yourself up through affirmation therapy. My first introduction to affirmation therapy came from a sales manager years ago who told us what to do just before we went in to make a sales call. "Pop your fist into your hand and shout aloud three times, 'Boy, am I enthusiastic!'" It seemed like a silly exercise at the time, but I learned that it worked. Subsequently I discovered why. You can play a benign trick on the unconscious mind this way. The unconscious mind responds to a message that it believes to be true by sending out affirmative messages to the entire nervous system.

- *Use humor.* The ability to see something funny in your misfortunes is an important coping skill. Begin by smiling. That's right. Physically put a smile on your face. You will discover that it's almost impossible to feel depressed when you are engaged in smiling. If you don't believe it, right now, put a big, silly smile on your face, and then try to feel depressed.

   The next step is stimulating laughter—at least a chuckle. If you can do something to make you laugh, you have taken a giant step toward defeating negative, defeatist attitudes. Laughter increases blood circulation, feeds oxygen to the brain, pumps out hormones that aid alertness, and releases pain-killing endorphins. Humorist/professional speaker Jim Pelley makes these suggestions about ways to put humor to work:

   1. Create a humor file that you fill with cartoons and clever sayings. Get it out when you're feeling depressed or doing stressful activities, like when you're put on hold on the phone. Instead of fuming, you can enjoy a chuckle or two.
   2. Use props, like a bird whistle, a silly cap, goofy-looking glasses, etc.
   3. Stand in front of a mirror and lead an enthusiastic cheer for yourself.
   4. Spend some time with someone who can make you laugh.
   5. Rent a funny video.
   6. Go to a big toy store. Watch the kids. Handle some of the toys yourself.
   7. Learn a magic trick.
   8. Find a new cartoon or one from your file and post it in a conspicuous place.
   9. Smile at five people you don't know.

   If some of these activities sound a bit ridiculous, don't worry about it. Go ahead and do them. The point is to be a bit ridiculous, and benefit from the experience.

- *Talk about your feelings with a trusted friend.* Don't divulge your innermost thoughts to just anyone, or to just any acquaintance. But if you know someone who isn't a gossip and who has good listening skills, just talking through your problem can be excellent therapy.

- *Yield to temptation.* Drop out of circulation for few hours or a few days. If you've successfully completed a project, take time to shift gears. If you've gone through a traumatic experience, take time to restore your equilibrium. One major TV personality occasionally gets so depressed that she has to go to bed. "I have a good cry," she says. "I cry till I can't cry anymore. I've found that it helps *not* to try to get out of it prematurely. So, I just wallow in self-pity. Eventually, I get sick and tired of it, and then I can be productive again." For her, a larger dose of the disease is its cure.

- *Do low-priority items on your list.* Do something that doesn't require a great deal of thought or willpower yet still needs to be done. If you've just had a political setback at the office, or if a hoped-for project wasn't funded, or if you missed a sale, or if you had a fight with a friend or family member, don't just sit around and mope. There are plenty of low-priority chores that you could tackle while you're in this kind of mood. If you've been putting off waxing the car, or straightening up your closet, or filing your photographs, or getting your financial records ready for income tax time, do that. The benefits are twofold. One, you'll be doing some things that really ought to get done eventually. Two, because you're active, you just may work your way out of the down mood. This tactic is particularly useful for people who do creative kinds of jobs. The mind may be tired but the body isn't. So bring body and mind into balance by doing some projects that require physical activity. You will find that you will be able to phase back into a higher-level priority sooner than you think. That's exactly what Jesse Slone, a workshop participant, does regularly, not just to get out of a slump. Here's what Slone told me: "Rank your tasks and do the second-hardest thing first, not the hardest. You'll do it, and do it fast."

- *Do something that you're good at.* If you're depressed because you've just had a failure, don't try something else that has high risk. Golf probably isn't a good idea, unless you're certain that you won't beat up on yourself afterward. Do something easy.

- *Do mental calisthenics.* No single tactic always works in a down mood. If you have to write a proposal, but it isn't working, just write anything. Doodle with words. The first few paragraphs or pages may eventually be thrown away. Simply getting started without thinking very much about what you're doing limbers up the mental muscles. You're like a football player getting ready to hit your opponent through pregame calisthenics and contact drills.

- *Force yourself to do something entirely different from your usual routine.* Jog, play tennis, or go to the mall. If these are customary activities, try something different.

- *Dress the part.* Wear an outfit with power colors or something bright and cheerful. When Ken Futch resigned his sales job at AT&T to become a consultant, trainer, and professional speaker, he was concerned that he might become sloppy about his work habits. So, he decided to adopt a practice that he has faithfully maintained ever since. Each morning, he walks down the stairs to the office in his residence—dressed the same way he would be dressed if he were going to work in the corporate world. Futch says he does it to be professional, to be ready for the unexpected invitation to meet a client for a meeting, and to get his mind ready for work. Getting ready physically is a good way to get ready mentally and emotionally.

- *Experiment with your diet.* Depression and efficiency-sapping moods can be the result of your bodily metabolism or improper diet. Hypothyroidism, hypoglycemia, anemia, or allergies can cause low energy. A physician can give you a test for these. But you can be your own physician in certain respects too. The best way to find out if certain foods affect your energy levels is to try an elimination diet. Eliminate one food after another until you find the offender. Later add back foods one at a time to see which reactivates the symptoms. You may not need to eliminate some of them entirely, but simply lessen the intake.

   Dairy products and wheat contain tryptophan, which is a natural sedative. Other offenders may be sugar-containing foods, alcoholic drinks, peanuts, corn, eggs, and soft drinks. An energy-rich diet includes dried beans and peas, raw nuts and seeds, fruits and vegetables, complex starches such as potatoes and sweet potatoes, rice, and potassium-filled foods such as leafy green vegetables and melons.[12]

- *Get some sunlight.* This old recommendation for sickly individuals has a sound scientific basis. Numerous studies have shown that people who are deprived of sunlight often experience mild to severe depression. Even artificial sunlight can be helpful. In Sweden, with its long, dark winters, physicians report a 75 percent success rate using artificial sunlight therapy.[13]

- *Pick a career that matches your temperament.* The most successful entrepreneurs make comments like, "I'm just naturally upbeat." "I am not easily discouraged." "I seem to have a lot of energy and can keep going when others stop." "I don't worry about setbacks very much." If this doesn't sound like you, perhaps entrepreneurial ventures aren't for you. A person who's not agreeable shouldn't go into public relations and a person who isn't just a bit skeptical shouldn't go into purchasing. You probably shouldn't go into commission sales if defeat knocks you down and keeps you down for long periods of time. The depression and anxiety may be too much for you. If you're a second-guesser and are constantly agonizing over decisions that you've made, you probably shouldn't go into management. Hiring and firing people and making tough decisions about which vendor to use or which plant to close may cause you too much anguish.

- *Develop a process for dealing with specific problems that trouble you.* Martin E. P. Seligman, author of *Learned Optimism*, recommends writing down the troublesome thought at the moment it occurs. Don't brood. Brooding is the mind's way of telling you not to forget about the worrisome subject. If you write it down, you've eliminated the main purpose that brooding has. When you write down the troublesome thought, Seligman suggests that you schedule a specific time for thinking about the problem. If you find yourself brooding about the issue prior to that specific time, do something physically distracting, like snapping a rubber band on your wrist or dashing cold water on your face while saying, "Stop! I'll think about that at nine this evening."[14]

❧

GIVE YOURSELF A BREAK

Economist and former U.S. Ambassador John Kenneth Galbraith once told me that we would be surprised and perhaps alarmed if we knew how many of the world's most important decisions had been made by people who desperately needed sleep. Galbraith was our ambassador to India when conflict broke out between that nation and China in the 1960s. He observed diplomats and military people making crucial decisions after going for many hours with little or no sleep. "It was a bit scary," he told me.

National leaders have often been criticized for taking too many breaks and vacations. However, taking a break or taking a nap is precisely what they probably need most. Churchill's frequent naps were legendary. He often worked late into the night, but he frequently stayed in bed until midday. Franklin D. Roosevelt once told his friend Hugh Johnson: "During my waking, working hours, I give the best in me....When time comes for rest, I can reflect that I could not have done it better if I had to do it all over again except for hindsight, which does not come at the same time as the problem. There is nothing left for me to do but to close my eyes and I am asleep."[15] Harry Truman had that same ability, former Secretary of State Dean Rusk told me. "He would make his decision, go home and go to sleep and never look back."

The tactic is valuable in other fields too. Famed animal trainer Gunther Gebel-Williams was always the first to be up and ready for work in the morning and the last to turn in at night. His "power naps" were legendary in the circus. He would even nap between costume changes—lie down flat on the floor and sleep. His wife told me, "Sometimes I get nervous when he's driving because I'm afraid he will take a power nap then."

It is possible to build up your endurance so that you can keep going when the body is extremely tired. But that can be safely done for only short periods. If you are working beyond your usual parameters for an extended time, you are creating a sleep deficit, which is just like a deficit in your bank balance that will need to be balanced.

If you find yourself snapping at people and making careless decisions, you'd better take a break. Rest. If you listen to your body and take a nap, you probably will be able to rapidly regain the ground that you lose during the break.

KNOW HOW LONG YOU CAN WAIT TO DO IT

If you want to book a cruise or a choice vacation spot during the peak holiday period, you must make a reservation well in advance. The rooms are usually fully booked and so are the flights weeks or months before the holiday time.

However, if you can be flexible and don't need to travel at peak times, you can often save substantial sums of money by waiting. In fact, a segment of the travel industry specializes in selling cruise tickets and tours at the last minute.

Some very successful people deliberately put off tasks. Some negotiators skillfully delay coming to a decision because they know their opponent is facing a deadline, and delay weakens their opponent's bargaining power. Some sellers don't return phone calls quickly as part of a strategy to show they aren't in a hurry to sell. And some very successful people just plain procrastinate. Oscar de la Renta told me that he tends to wait until the point of no return. He thinks waiting that long actually helps make his creative juices flow.

It's risky business, though, being a procrastinator. If you decide to do it, here are some tips. Start the project early. Take the first step. Some skillful procrastinators write down their preliminary ideas or make a few sketches and then file them for later use. Then while these individuals seem to be absorbed with other projects, their unconscious mind is chugging away, producing information and concepts and new ideas. And it's doing editing too, discarding flawed or superfluous ideas.

Charles Brady has built Invesco into one of the premier financial management firms in the world. But Brady doesn't use a
sophisticated system to get his projects done. He told me that at
any one time he will be working on six or seven major projects,
some stretching out over several months or even a year or two.
As material comes across his desk daily, he glances at it and if
it's relevant, puts it in one of the six or seven stacks. Other
items, like correspondence are acted on immediately, sent away
to the files, or dealt with by his executive secretary. Brady has
constructed a special place in his cabinet for each of the six or
seven stacks. When it's time to take action on one of the six or
seven projects, Brady goes to that stack and begins to work
through it.

This is a variation of a technique that I've used for years. I
begin a new project by assigning it a manila folder, and as I come
across relevant material, I put it in the folder. As thoughts occur
to me or as comments are made to me that might be pertinent,
these get written down and subsequently put in the folder. I tear
out articles from magazines and place them in the file.

Sometimes it's amazing what happens when you put things
off. Columnist Russell Baker has described the panic he sometimes feels when he approaches a deadline: "Desperation is the
newspaperman's normal state of mind. Deadlines do that to him.
He lives in a world where time is forever running out....On his
inner clock, it is always two minutes to midnight and the work
only half done, maybe not even started yet, and he must
absolutely have it ready for the printer before the bell tolls,
whether he has anything to write or not."[16]

When Baker was asked to write a regular column for *The New
York Times,* he felt elated at first. But within weeks, the dream
had turned to a nightmare. The dreaded villain of the nightmare
was the column, which demanded he write whether he felt like it
or not.

Gradually, Baker learned to refuse to think about the column
until the moment he had to write it. He found that in between
columns, his mind was storing away ideas for later use.
Sometimes he would come right to the zero hour and think, "This
is the day I finally can't write the thing before deadline. This is

the day I go out the window." But always at that "moment of ultimate desperation," his mind came up with something that it had filed away "when it should have been idling."[17]

It's not clear why waiting to get started causes the creative juices to flow. Perhaps knowing that there is very little room for error and no further possibility of delay concentrates the mind and raises the energy level. Energy is essential for good work. Highly creative people use various kinds of tactics to get their energy level up and keep it up. Delay is one such tactic. Coming face-to-face with a deadline you're not ready for can set the heart to pumping, the adrenalin flowing.

For years, I advised college students: "Don't wait until the last minute to start studying for an exam. Don't wait until the last minute to write your paper." And I have seen abundant proof that this is good advice. I cannot tell you how many points I have deducted through the years for papers that were turned in late because a typist got sick, a printer jammed, a computer bombed, or a close relative died. (I am sure that exam time must be a very dangerous time for close relatives of college students. So many of them seem to expire then.)

But I must confess that I have seen some students thrive on procrastination. Some of the very best papers I ever received were done by students who worked all night long and, in effect, stood on the edge of a cliff. (Some of the worst ones were done that way, too.)

A student once told me she didn't think my class was fair. She had studied every day and her two classmates hadn't. They had waited until the last night to cram, she said, and they had made better grades than she. I replied that perhaps she had studied at too leisurely a pace. Because she knew the test was far away, she had not studied intensely. She had spent more *time* than they had. They had spent more *energy*.

Samuel Johnson wrote, "Depend upon it, Sir, when a man knows he is to be hanged in a fortnight, it concentrates his mind wonderfully."

Living close to the edge can sometimes improve, rather than diminish, quality. But be warned that people who live on the edge of a cliff sometimes fall off.

🐌

BEWARE OF PARKINSON'S LAW

It is the busiest man who has time to spare. —ANONYMOUS

With this proverb as a touchstone, British historian C. Northcote Parkinson analyzed why large organizations become bloated and lethargic. Parkinson formulated a law that reads as follows: "Work expands so as to fill the time available for its completion." Parkinson's law explains why organizations become much larger than they need to, but it also explains one reason why individuals become inefficient. They allow too much time for the proposed project.

In a delightful little sketch, Parkinson describes an elderly lady who spends the entire day dispatching a postcard to her niece.

> An hour will be spent in finding the postcard, another in hunting for the spectacles, half an hour in search for an address, an hour and a quarter in composition, and twenty minutes in deciding whether or not to take an umbrella when going to the mailbox on the next street. The total effort that would occupy a busy man for three minutes all told may in this fashion leave another person prostrate after a day of doubt, anxiety, and toil.[18]

Parkinson concluded that there is little or no relationship between the work to be done and the amount of resources that may be devoted to it. "The thing to be done swells in importance and complexity in a direct ratio with the time to be spent."

You would think that giving yourself lots and lots of time to do what you need to do would improve the quality of your work. But that's not always the case. Having a lot of time may make you sloppy, unmotivated, and inefficient. There may be a great drop-off in intensity. I once heard a child psychologist report on one of her clients who was having difficulty in school maintaining a "C" average. The youngster was taking only the minimum number of courses. The psychologist surprised the parents by recommending that the student take more courses, not fewer. To the surprise of the student and her parents, the student's grades in all the courses improved rather than declined. What happened was that the student had to learn to become more efficient. And that stepped up her energy level.

Much of my career has been spent on university campuses, where I have observed the work habits of academic scholars. Academics tend to believe that nothing really good can be done quickly. This often is true, but it sometimes is an excuse for sloth and procrastination. I know of one instance in which a university professor at a major university was contacted by a competent science writer at a large newspaper who needed a two- or three-sentence quote. The quote wasn't about something controversial or revolutionary. He needed only a simple description of the field the professor was in. The professor told the writer it would take him at least a week to compose the quote. The writer needed the quote that afternoon. The professor couldn't believe the writer could make such a ridiculous request, and the writer couldn't believe the professor required such a ridiculous amount of time.

I have often been amazed at what a fine journalist can write—for all the world to see—in just a few minutes. How can they do it? Because they have to. And this fact doesn't apply to just journalists. The great jazz musician and composer Duke Ellington once said, "Without a deadline, I can't finish nothin'."

Obviously you can take this idea too far. You can allow too little time for careful preparation and high-quality work. The trick is to find a healthy balance. Only experience can tell you how much time you can allow for projects.

When I was approached by a publisher about writing a book, *The Achievement Factors,* I was asked how long I would need to write the first draft.[19] I told them two years. Back came the reply, "If you can complete it in six months, we will put the book on our A list and give it maximum publicity." I plunged into the project and surprised myself by completing the manuscript in six months. (Actually, the interviews on which the manuscript was based took place over a 12-year period.) If the publisher had said two years, it probably would have taken two years.

LEARN HOW TO SHIFT INTO THE SURGE MODE

High achievers from many different fields speak of being able to regulate their intensity—of being able to phase in and out of an intense state. Some people call this intense state the "surge mode."

Using the surge mode is a bit like using a passing gear in a car. Normally, when you're driving, you don't give a lot of conscious thought to putting your foot on the accelerator or on the brake. But sometimes you require an extra burst of power to get out of one lane and into another. Then you need extra power, and you "floorboard" it. That's what the surge mode is.

There are many illustrations of high achievers using the surge mode. Mozart preferred to write music for an hour or so every morning when he got up. But when a piece was demanded, he would work day and night without sleep, sometimes seemingly mesmerized by the task.

Isaac Newton made three of his greatest discoveries during two years of virtually uninterrupted thought, study, and experimentation. Mark Twain wrote six of his best books—*The Adventures of Huckleberry Finn, The Adventures of Tom Sawyer, Roughing It, A Connecticut Yankee in King Arthur's Court, Life on the Mississippi,* and *The Prince and the Pauper*—during only two summers. He would write an entire day at a time, day after day. His daughter, Claire, remembers that he would come out in a white linen suit, with a pile of pads of paper under his arm. He would joke with his family and then head off toward the study. There he would spend the entire day, sometimes eating only one meal.[20]

The surge mode is especially apparent among creative people, such as scientists, writers, musicians, and designers. They will gather all the parts of the project together—the notes, the rough ideas, the books, the research, the sketches—and spread it all before them on a desk or table. Then they dive in and don't stop until a major part or sometimes all of the project is done.

It is really much more efficient to do huge chunks of work at a time than it is to start and stop a hundred times. The quality of the finished product is better too because it is more cohesive and has fewer seams.

How do you get into the surge mode other than simply plunging in and not stopping? One way is to conjure up a mental image of a great triumph if you do it, or a great failure if you don't.

8

Avoid Procrastination

DO IT NOW

The best time to plant a tree was 20 years ago.
The second best time is now. —CHINESE PROVERB

Suzanne Caygill has helped some of the nation's most successful people design their homes and wardrobes. She's an internationally recognized color consultant who believes color is the key to unlocking a personality. That concept, which she's researched and elaborated through the years, has brought her renown and hundreds of clients.

How does she deal with all the demands on her time that such success has brought? Caygill told me that she follows a rule she learned from her grandmother. If she has a job she needs to do, she does it immediately. Her grandmother was a superb seamstress, who attacked the job with a sense of urgency, and she drilled that philosophy into her young granddaughter.

Too many people waste time "commencing to proceed to get started," Caygill says. They spend so much time *preparing* to do something that they often have no time left to do it. She says it's a mistake to spend lots and lots of time fretting over the purchase of a suit or an accessory or a painting. Follow your first impulse, she says.

The prominent designer Oscar de la Renta gives the same advice. When I asked him to provide some advice for women who go shopping for a dress, here's what he said: "You should have a reaction immediately, one way or another. If you have to think about a dress to say you like it or not, then the dress doesn't really mean anything. I make up my mind very, very fast about things, because anything that takes long thinking doesn't really interest me."

If you've been congratulating yourself that you are slow and deliberate, cautious and prudent, you may actually be following a practice that simply wastes a lot of time.

What about other areas, decisions that require research? Shouldn't impulsive decisions be avoided then? Usually?

But even in research it's possible to put off closure too long. Thomas R. Williams, former chairman of First Wachovia Corporation, told me that many young people who come into banking have a terribly difficult time knowing when to stop researching and when to take action. He says fact finding is important, but there comes a time when you have to stop fact finding and start working toward a solution.

In one of my presentations, I made the comment that engineers are taught to make decisions and not to try forever to find a perfect solution. Instead, they look for the best possible solution. In fact, they have an expression for it. Engineers call it "freezing the design." What it means is that they must *freeze*—make a decision about—the design by a certain date.

After the presentation, several executives who work with engineers came up to correct me. "If you left engineers alone, they would never come up with a design," they told me. "Good managers force engineers to freeze the design." Engineers are, indeed, taught to know how to get closure by a certain date. But it is a management function to tell what the specific date will be.

"Doing it now" is a good tactic even if you're not in charge of a project, if you're the delegatee instead of the delegator. "The best way to get noticed and loved before you're brilliant at your job is to do everything instantly," says Cosmopolitan editor Helen Gurley Brown. "A boss may give you five 'instantlies' and you have to decide which to do first, second, and so on, but get on with it all." Of course, it's a perfectly reasonable request to ask which of the instantlies is absolutely critical.[21]

Here are some ways to do it now. When you're preparing a travel reimbursement report, prepare that report as soon as you return to the office. You will probably spend less than a few minutes on the entire task. But if you wait six weeks and have four or five more trips to sort out, you will spend much more time than if you had done it on the spot. If you're a graduate student, sit down and finish the dissertation. Don't try to write the greatest dissertation ever written on the subject. Just do the best possible job you can do, and get started now.

Tom Johnson, president of CNN, told me that he tries to turn around every letter and phone call within 24 hours. Dick Biggs just completed his first book entitled *If Life Is a Balancing Act, Why Am I So Clumsy?* Biggs told me recently that I gave him some advice that helped him write the book. "What was the advice I gave you," I asked, because I honestly didn't remember what I had told him. "You told me, 'Just Do It.' And I did."

Goethe wrote:

> What you can do, or dream you can do, begin it,
>
> Boldness has genius, power and magic in it.
>
> Only engage, and then the mind grows heated–
>
> Begin it, and the work will be completed![22]

FINISH IT NOW

Andy Rooney, of *60 Minutes* fame, told me that his hobby is furniture making. But he admitted that he has a bad habit. He will find a great pattern, buy some fine wood, and will work it until it is 90 percent completed. Then he will put it aside, perhaps without sanding it or staining it.

I used to have that same affliction until I realized what a time-waster it is. I would start projects and do a major portion of the work. Then I would put it aside for one reason or another, instead of pushing the entire project across the finish line. The excuse to quit was tiredness—mental exhaustion, perhaps. I would quit, with the promise that I would come back to it another day. I had file folders bulging with almost-completed projects. Gradually I have learned to push myself to do that final 10 percent while I was at it—instead of putting the project away in an almost-completed state.

Here are the advantages. If you finish a project while you have it out, you save time putting it away, then getting it out again and having to go through the "Now, where was I?" process. Some projects, like books, just can't be completed at one sitting. But more projects can be completed at a stretch than you realize. It just takes the will to finish what you start.

ॐ

MAKE THE UNPLEASANT PHONE CALL FIRST: THE JACKIE WARD RULE

Jackie Ward is president and chief executive officer of Computer Generation, Inc., a company that designs and produces computer software for the hotel industry. Several years ago, she introduced me to a tactic that's so useful that I have appreciatively called it the Jackie Ward rule.

Here's the background for the tactic. If you know that you need to make a phone call that you anticipate will be unpleasant, what are you likely to do? That's right: put it off. You are also likely to put off a meeting that is likely to be unpleasant.

But that's not what Jackie Ward does. Here's what she told me: "I address all of my problem situations immediately. I'm not going to waste time dreading them....I want them over with, behind me, so I can get on with the part of the day that is enjoyable and productive. I deal with the unpleasant situations immediately. I just cannot bear to have dread things hanging over me."

What Ward does is counterintuitive. Intuitively we try to avoid pain, and that includes unpleasant phone calls and meetings. However, you don't really avoid pain by putting it off. Whenever you put off dealing with a dreaded situation, you probably will fret over it and replay various versions of the future encounter in your mind. Doing that can be stressful, tiring, and even painful. So dealing with a potentially painful experience immediately may actually abbreviate the unpleasantness.

Another reason Jackie Ward's tactic makes sense is because a fairly large number of dreaded encounters turn out to be less painful than we thought they would be. Often you can't know for sure how unpleasant things will be until you make the contact. The longer you put off the dreaded phone call, the longer you have to live with dread.

So do what Jackie Ward does. Address the problem situation immediately, make the dreaded phone call. Then, you can move on to more enjoyable activities.

❧

EXCEPTIONS TO THE JACKIE WARD RULE

There are three big exceptions to the Jackie Ward rule. One exception I learned from financial planner Gretchen Paprocki. If you are in sales, she advises, avoid any unpleasant experiences early in the day. Try for the warm, fuzzy, happy experience first. Paprocki understands that successful selling depends on self-confidence and enthusiasm. So don't make the unpleasant phone call or have the unpleasant meeting first *if you are in sales*.

The second exception I learned from the late Rev. A. J. Holt, a Baptist minister. Don't do the dreaded thing first if you're planning the agenda for a meeting. Do easy, friendly stuff first, he taught me. Then attack the tough issue.

Dr. Holt conducted a business meeting as skillfully as anyone I've ever seen. He always had an agenda for a meeting. And, he always took the easy items first. These would be matters that did-n't require much discussion and would almost certainly get a unanimous vote if a vote was required.

Holt did his homework prior to the meeting so that he had a good sense of which items would, and would not, arouse controversy. If there was an item that might require extensive discussion—like a change in the bylaws of the organization—he would save that item until the very last. Had he dealt with that item first, all the other small items would probably not have been dealt with at all. And the participants would have left the meeting feeling that not much was accomplished. However, by working through lots of small, relatively unimportant items prior to the big one, people had a sense of accomplishment by the time they took on the big task.

Holt also made sure that potentially troublesome items were first dealt with in committees prior to the big meeting, and that influential people were on those committees. The committees did the spade work prior to the meeting and the influential people on the committees carried enough weight to create a consensus.

The third exception is when you're negotiating: Don't start with the toughest item first. See if you can find agreement on small, easy items at the beginning. Doing this generates goodwill, plus it requires a time investment from the other party. And every skilled negotiator knows that the longer some people invest in a transaction, the less willing they will be to walk away from it without some kind of a deal.

This tactic isn't limited to conducting meetings. It's a valid principle to put to work in exercise programs and volunteer projects as well. Tackling the easy stuff first helps build momentum, creates goodwill, and fosters a spirit of cooperation so that when you eventually reach tough items, they will seem less formidable.

This tactic works for all sorts of leaders. If you've just come to a position, instead of taking on a high-risk project right away, attempt a project that has little risk of failure. Then take on another low-risk project. Gradually, you will gain the reputation for being successful at what you do, and people will be more likely to follow you, less likely to resist you. Eventually you will get to the dreaded tasks, but then you will come at them with more resources, more enthusiasm, more experience, and more followers than had you tackled them at the beginning.

ELIMINATE OVERDRAFTS

Have you ever received a notice with a real deadline like this?

LAST DATE WITHOUT PENALTY: MAY 1ST. APPLICATION SHOULD BE MAILED BY APRIL 1ST TO ENSURE YOUR RECEIVING DECAL BY MAY 1ST.

Most of us have. In the state where I live, it's possible to order a car tag by mail. The other alternative is to physically go to an office and stand in line. To use the first option, it's necessary to mail in the forms by May 1. Yet what will happen the last day of April? Every year throngs of people line up at the designated office. These individuals seem to be intelligent, but they have to spend long hours in line because they did not take advantage of the option of mailing in their payment on time.

Most of them can read, so that's not the problem. In fact, if you conducted a poll of the people in line, you probably would hear a litany of excuses: "I didn't have the money then." (Yet, somehow they have found a way to have it now.) "I couldn't get away from the office." (But they can now.) "My mail went to the wrong address." (The notices go out months in advance.) "I lost my notice." (But they didn't call to request another.) The main reason most of these people are in line is more honest: "I just let it slip up on me."

Mild forms of procrastination are benign. In fact, we have already seen that procrastination can sometimes be used as a stimulus. But a missed deadline that requires you to pay costly penalties or waste hours of time is sheer, unhappy folly. It's like an overdraft in your checking account. For example, if you don't pay your traffic tickets in cities with tough enforcement measures, like Denver, Boston, Washington, D.C., or New York City, it can be a costly experience. If you get caught, plan to spend a lot of time getting your car unbooted or claiming it at some God-forsaken impounding area. Your "overdraft" will cost you the fine, penalties, plus your valuable time. So pay your tickets and taxes and fees promptly. Don't put yourself in a position in which you have to pay costly penalties—in money and time.

9

Avoid Time-Wasting Activities

IF IT'S NOT WORTH DOING, BE SURE NOT TO DO IT

Don't be the slave of your in-box. Just because something's there doesn't mean you have to do it. —MALCOLM S. FORBES, JR.

Playwright Neil Simon says the way he decides whether or not to develop an idea into a play is by asking, "If I were to write this play, and fulfill all of its promise, on each and every page, and carry the play and its characters to their richest potential, just how good a play can this be?" The answer, he says, sometimes is: "Not bad. A good play but not worth a year or two of your life." If that's the answer. Simon doesn't do it.[23]

Unfortunately, most people don't begin to ask this kind of question until they are pretty far along in their careers. That's probably because when we are young we sometimes don't realize just how long projects that we begin can really take or how little time we really have.

That was certainly true early in my career. Just after I became department head at a large university, a statewide scientific organization asked me to present a paper at their annual meeting.

Thinking this was the politic thing to do, I accepted, and devoted a considerable amount of time to the project.

What a disappointment the presentation turned out to be. The only people who showed up at my session were the other people on the program: a total of four.

Chastened thus, I made a resolution that day never to say yes so easily again. Not long afterward, I received an invitation from the same organization to develop the paper I had presented into an article to be published in their journal that nobody read. I declined.

However, I discovered that a number of faculty members from my university made such presentations and also wrote papers year after year. They dutifully listed these activities on their résumés. One day I commented to a friend at another university, "At least these people are doing something, and that's better than doing nothing."

"You're wrong," he said. "It's worse than doing nothing. They think they're doing *something* when, in fact, they're doing *nothing*. That's worse than doing nothing."

He was right. In fact there are four good reasons never to do anything not worth doing:

- Things not worth doing can delude you into thinking you've actually accomplished something. Like my colleagues who listed on their résumés papers that nobody heard or read, you may proudly feel self-congratulatory about useless efforts.

- Things not worth doing divert time and energy from things that are worth doing. Much of life is a zero-sum game. Resources that are devoted to one activity are taken away from another activity. Everything spent on something not worth doing could be spent on something useful.

- Things not worth doing take on a life of their own. The sociologist Max Weber observed that the mere regularity of an activity gradually gives it the quality of "oughtness." After a while, people will say, "We ought not to let this die. We've been doing it a long time." Many organizations, publications, or activities should never have been begun in the first place. But they continue because people have grown accustomed to them, derive part of their identity from them, and would feel guilt-stricken if they let them die.

■ Things not worth doing have babies. Do something not worth doing and soon you will need to form a committee to provide for its oversight. Eventually you will need subcommittees, officers, handbooks, and guidelines, plus annual retreats to learn how better to do things not worth doing. One day a wealthy person will die and leave money to endow a university chair to teach the thing not worth doing. The possibilities are endless and frightening.

You may have little choice in the matter. You may be very junior and powerless. But whenever you have a choice, apply the Neil Simon litmus test. Ask yourself, "If I—or we—develop this idea to it's fullest potential, is it really worth doing?" If the answer is no, be sure not to do it.

🙚

DON'T QUIT TOO SOON

I make a list of things I like to play with: a film on the Amazon, on Haiti, building the windship. I try, and I don't get the money. I try again and I don't get the money. After 10 years, I get the money.
—JACQUES COUSTEAU

If you visit the Cairo Museum, you will see absolutely dazzling objects taken from the tomb of Tutankhamen. Much of the second floor of that huge building is filled with glittering treasures—jewelry of gold and precious stones, ornaments, gold and alabaster vessels, chariots, coffins of ivory and gold with workmanship that could not be surpassed today. That incredible treasure might still be in the ground were it not for Howard Carter's decision to dig just one more day.

During the winter of 1922, Carter had almost given up hope that he would ever find the lost tomb of the young pharaoh. His sponsor was about to withdraw support. In his autobiography, Carter wrote these words:

> This was to be our final season in The Valley. Six full seasons we had excavated there, and season after season had drawn a blank; we had worked for months at a stretch and found nothing, and only an excavator knows how desperately depressing that can be; we had almost made up our minds that we were beaten, and were preparing to leave The Valley and try our luck elsewhere; and then—hardly had we set hoe to ground in our last despairing effort than we made a discovery that far exceeded our wildest dreams.

Howard Carter's "final despairing effort" made headlines around the world. He had discovered the only intact tomb of a pharaoh found in modern times.

One of the biggest time-wasters is quitting too soon. Too often people do 90 percent of the work, but fail to do the final 10 percent that would take them to success. They lose their initial investment, not to mention the joy that comes from discovering a treasure with that last despairing effort.

Many times a person will take a new job or begin to acquire a new skill and then quit in discouragement just before the payoff begins. In any new job, there's usually a difficult period when you know less than anyone around you. At first everything is a bit of a struggle, but after a while, tasks that at first were stressful can be done effortlessly.

You may remember trying to learn a new language. If you quit after a few months, chances are you didn't learn enough to enjoy the skill you were acquiring. After a few more months or years, you probably would have been able to carry on conversations and read books and newspapers. In many areas of life, people quit before they cross the critical threshold between tedium and pleasure, between struggle and success.

Charles Schulz told me that he wasn't an overnight success, even after he sold his famous comic strip: "'Peanuts' did not take the world by storm immediately. It was a long grind. It took 'Peanuts' about four years to attract nationwide attention, but it took ten years to become really entrenched."

❧
KNOW WHEN TO CUT YOUR LOSSES

If at first you don't succeed, try again. Then quit.
No use being a damn fool about it. —W. C. FIELDS

Nobel laureate Linus Pauling told me that the mark of a good researcher is knowing which ideas to follow up and which to throw away. "Otherwise, you can waste a lot of time on bad ideas."

Sooner or later you will find yourself in a situation that requires you to cut your losses. The line of research you've been following may have led to a cul-de-sac. Should you try one more experiment? You've invested an enormous amount of time and energy in a transaction or relationship. Despite your best efforts, the situation has grown progressively worse. You have tried, but nothing has come of your efforts except excuses and more promises. You have discussed and negotiated and compromised but the relationship seems determined to go downhill. The natural tendency is to want to make one more effort because you have invested so much in it already. What to do?

There are several fundamental questions to help decide when to hold, when to fold, when to keep trying, and when to cut losses:

- *Can you obtain additional information?*   One of the best steps you can take is to seek additional information or re-examine old information from a new perspective. For this, you may need to hire a skilled mechanic, technician, or consultant. If a relationship is not going the way you think it should, perhaps you can gain information from people who have dealt in the past with the person or company in question or been in similar situations.

  Nobel laureate Francis Crick told me that a capable and forthright colleague was the single most important resource a researcher could have. In sales a seasoned pro can often advise a rookie when it's time to forget about a prospect and move on to another.

- *Are there impenetrable barriers?* Have you reached a point that some people call the "walk-away position"? Generally, the walk-away position is reached when further engagement would result in a major loss for either or both parties.

  Recognizing which problems are deal breakers and which can be resolved can save much time and pain. Often people aren't aware that an issue is a deal breaker because they are unwilling to look for it or ask the right kinds of questions. Even when they recognize a deal breaker for what it is, they may try to pretend it doesn't exist. Denial often simply puts off the inevitable.

  Look for deal breakers early in the game. Zero in on nonnegotiable items. If there is a fundamental conflict over something that means a great deal to you, and if you are convinced that neither of you will change, you have reached the walk-away position. Walk away.

  The impenetrable barrier may be built into the structure. You may be trying to advance in a company that will always choose its top people from family members or from a particular ethnic group or gender. If you're not from those categories, you probably need to move to where success is possible.

- *How big is the potential payoff?* If you're a Howard Carter looking for the lost tomb of a pharaoh, you can afford to look for years. The potential payoff is tremendous. But if you're a salesperson, you can't afford to spend many hours on a prospect who, at best, will produce only a few dollars of business.

- *How much will it cost to do the project or keep the relationship going?* If you are trying to decide whether to repair the office copier or purchase a new one, write down how much you have already spent during the previous year on the present machine. How much can you reasonably expect to spend repairing the copier during the next 24 months? Be sure to factor in how much it costs when the machine is down. How much is the frustration worth? Estimate what it costs to send your work out or wait until the machine is repaired. And then factor in just how effective the machine is when it *is* working. Do people have to stand in line even when it's working at peak efficiency?

Some simple calculations may tell you that even if you do invest the time and money repairing the old machine, you won't get what you really want.

- *How deep are your pockets?* If you don't have deep pockets, there are some games you shouldn't play. The Corning Company could afford to spend millions of dollars and wait years before it made a penny from its fiber optics research. Eventually the payoff was enormous, but Corning had to wait for a long time to see it. You might have a great idea, but it may take too many resources for you to bring it to fruition. Try to negotiate a partnership or a buyout or walk away.

- *What are the patterns?* If you're trying to decide whether to continue a romantic, business, or social relationship, there's probably something about the relationship that's bothering you or you wouldn't be questioning it. Perhaps it's a realtor who hasn't shown your listing as many times as you would like, or it's a friend who's exploded in rage two or three times, or a colleague who promised to do something for you, but didn't. Should you give the person another chance? Should you turn the other cheek?

   Make some targeted inquiries. Find out how the individual or the company has performed with others in the past. Determine whether the disappointing experience was typical or an exception. Has this particular realtor taken listings before and then done nothing with them? Has this friend had tantrums in the past? Does this colleague make it a practice to promise more than he actually does? If you had asked these questions before beginning the relationship, you might not be having to ask them now. But better to ask them late than to continue in a costly relationship that will revert to type. One of my favorite folk sayings is, "You haven't learned anything from a mule that kicks you twice."

- *Is there a hidden agenda?* Some playing fields aren't level. Some decks aren't full. Some dice don't roll right. Most books on time management don't mention this topic. Yet, millions of hours are misspent each year on applications, projects, and competitions in which virtually all the participants have no chance whatsoever of succeeding. The interviews are just for show. The search is wired. An insider has already been chosen. The effective time tactician knows and uses defensive tactics, not just offensive ones.

What do you do if you suspect a hidden agenda, a wired search? Do all the research you can. Don't leap to conclusions. A search may seem to be wired, but the insider is only favored, not guaranteed success. If you make a strong showing, you may win. However, the players may be too shrewd for you to find out what is really happening. When you are reasonably sure you cannot win, no matter how hard you try, make your exit. Don't exhaust your resources in a dishonest game.

KNOW WHEN TO LEAVE WELL ENOUGH ALONE

You can hope for too much. Sometimes good enough is good enough. In Herbert Simon's autobiography, the world-renowned scientist says, "The best can be the enemy of the good."[24] You can dissipate so much time and effort dreaming about perfection that you don't have time to do anything very well.

Actress Peggy Ashcroft once told director Norris Houghton that she had discovered from her own experiences and from working with some of the greats, like Gielgud and Olivier, that "there are some great roles…which no one can play at full strength from beginning to end. One simply hopes that one can hit the peaks as often as one has the strength."[25]

Bobby Jones arrived at that same conclusion. He did what no other golfer has ever done: win the Grand Slam of golf, which included winning the United States Open, the United States Amateur, the British Open, and the British Amateur. Here's what he said: "It is a fact that I never did any real amount of winning until I learned to adjust my ambitions to more reasonable prospects shot by shot, and to strive for a rate of performance that was consistently good and reliable, rather than placing my hopes upon the accomplishments of a series of brilliant sallies."[26]

Bobby Jones did not reach that understanding easily. He had to fight hard against the temptation to push himself beyond his ability. During the early days of his golf career, he was always striving to hit the perfect shot, and when he didn't, he would break clubs and start yelling and sometimes even leave the course. He had such a temper that many golfers wouldn't play with him. Only gradually did he learn that once you hit a bad shot, it is over and you must strive to make the next shot as good as possible.

Sometimes perfection is worth striving for. Letters that go out of your office ought not to have any misspellings or faulty grammar. And let us hope that the people who make parachutes, condoms, and aircraft landing gears have a commitment to perfection. However, sometimes perfection is not worth the time it takes, even when it's attainable.

Successful time management depends on knowing when perfection is worth striving for and when to leave well enough alone. Sometimes you simply must go on to the next project, hit the next ball, or put the proposal in the mail.

Many of the projects and tasks that you have to do are a lot like running hurdles. You aren't supposed to knock over the hurdles, but there's no bonus for clearing them by an extra margin either. All you really have to do is get over them.

By analogy, if the project you're working on requires you to clear a large number of hurdles in a comparatively brief time, you will wear yourself out expending too much energy on the first hurdles and having no strength left for the last ones. And it slows you down, too. The best hurdlers clear the hurdles, but just barely.

That point is made in Allen N. Schoonmaker's survival manual for college students. Schoonmaker advises students to jump the obstacles by the barest possible margin so that energy is saved for the ones ahead. Graduate students who ignore the basic requirements for the degree, like passing a course in statistics, will never get a degree, no matter how creative they may be in other courses. Schoonmaker tells about one of his students at Berkeley who enjoyed research, was a hard worker, and was good at what he did, "but he fell over one of the obstacles, and was dragged off the course—after publishing 25 articles."[27]

Schoonmaker's observations are based on what happens in a special world, the world of the graduate student. But the same basic principle that he mentions applies to many other fields. If you take on unmanageable tasks, treat smallish projects as though they were destined for the Louvre, jump hurdles as you would the high jump, you will fail and that failure will injure your self-confidence and hurt your reputation.

This advice seems to discount the value of high-quality work. That's not true. In most instances, quality is what the customer wants. You might produce the world's finest fountain pen, costing thousands of dollars, but if the customer wants a good serviceable ballpoint that can be thrown away after being used, you've wasted time and other resources producing the expensive pen.

Your customer may not want you to spend a great deal of time on just one part of a project but will want you to do all parts adequately. Your manager (i.e., the "customer") may want you to simply scribble your reaction directly on a memo instead of drafting a long, studied reply to it. The trick is to find out what is really wanted by the customer. That's an all-important time tactic and a survival tactic as well.

❧
BECOME DECISIVE

Knowing how to decide if, how, and when to cut losses or leave well enough alone are all a part of the larger process of knowing how to make decisions. Not being able to make decisions can be a huge time-waster. Some people go into a tailspin whenever they are confronted with a choice.

Sound decision making has a basic structure. There is a sequence that good decision makers go through. Some individuals have refined it into an art form. But it takes practice. In fact, good management programs provide opportunities for initiates to develop skill at making decisions by making decisions.

Alan Weiss believes it is essential to understand and use the basic sequence of decision making. "Decisions should be made by first understanding the objective, then looking at alternatives, and then considering risk," Weiss says. "No matter what kind of bells and whistles you put on that, that's the basic sequence. People who lack these processes are knee-deep in content, and they waste tremendous amounts of time."

Work at becoming more decisive. Assimilate the decision-making model into your time tactics repertoire. Do some reading on the subject. Get input from good decision makers and learn from them. Watch how they do it. Practice making decisions with non-critical projects and evaluate the results. I've learned that it helps to write down what the alternatives are, list the plusses and minuses for each alternative, and assign weights to each plus or minus. There are usually plusses and minuses associated with any decision you have to make. Good decision making involves knowing or anticipating what they are and assessing how important the plusses and minuses will be.

I can recall instances when I was amazed how easy a decision became after I went through this process—on paper. Prior to doing it, the problem seemed tough.

Some very good people say they make decisions intuitively. They rely on gut feeling and instinct. I personally think that what seems like intuition to a highly successful person is really a decision rooted in deep knowledge. They know so much about a subject or have done something so long that the decision is habitual. I don't discount true intuition and gut instinct. I just wouldn't rely on them all the time. Learn the process of decision making and perfect it. It can save you huge chunks of time.

DON'T FINISH EVERY BOOK THAT YOU START

Some books are to be tasted, others to be swallowed, and some few to be chewed and digested: that is, some books are to be read only in parts, others to be read, but not curiously, and some few to be read wholly, and with diligence and attention. —FRANCIS BACON[28]

Francis Bacon's rule is a variation of the two preceding tactics, which involve cutting losses and avoiding doing anything that's not worth doing. Whether you're reading a book, watching a movie, or participating in an organization, you need not feel that you have to stay with something just because you happened to begin it. You may grow bored with a book or a movie, or a course of action, or you may outgrow it.

Don't feel you have to read or see everything. Many people feel guilty about the books that they started and never finished. They shouldn't. Very few books should be read in their entirety. Even those written by the most skillful authors have weak sections mixed with the strong. So, don't feel that you have a flawed character if you don't finish every book that you start.

Just because you paid for a book or newspaper or magazine doesn't mean that you must read it in order to avoid wasting money. Your time is a nonrenewable resource. The money you spent isn't. If a movie isn't good during the first five minutes, it generally will not improve. Film and TV producers generally try to put their best material at the front in order to grab the audience. If the best isn't good, what follows will be worse. That principle may not be as true for plays as it is for movies. Playwrights know that the audience for a play is usually a captive audience, and they may begin the story slowly, letting it unfold gradually.

Avoiding books and articles not worth reading can increase your reading speed up to 50,000 words per minute, according to a claim by CareerTrack's Jimmy Calano and Jeff Salzman: "All you have to do is recognize, within one minute, that a particular 50,000-word book does not suit your purposes, and decide not to read it."[29]

Another approach to avoid reading everything is to take advantage of synopses of books and articles in publications like *Communication Briefings, Bottom Line Personal,* and *Boardroom Reports* that summarize books and articles. The same service is available on several audiocassette programs.

A variation of this approach is to create a network of reviewers. The top executives in one large corporation (ALAGAS Corporation) regularly write and share reviews of books that they feel their colleagues will find interesting or useful. Each review reports the main ideas of the book or article. The practice was started by the CEO of the company, who is an avid reader and wanted his top people exposed to important ideas.

Don't feel that you have to know everything. Information has expanded so greatly that acquiring universal knowledge is no longer a doable task. For years I felt it was my duty as a university professor to try keep up with everything that was going on in the world, including politics, sports, the arts, business, and, of course, my own area of the social sciences. I was an "information junkie." I have reluctantly concluded that trying to know everything about everything is a vice, not a virtue. It keeps you from gaining a sure grip on any one subject.

Don't feel that you have to keep doing something that no longer means anything to you. You may have outgrown it or the people who do it. Your growth can often be measured by the activities you no longer do, the organizations you are no longer a member of, and the friends you no longer have. Ralph Waldo Emerson said it well: "A foolish consistency is the hobgoblin of little minds, adored by little statesmen and philosophers and divines. With consistency, a great soul has simply nothing to do."[30]

ès

DON'T BE PENNY-WISE AND HOURS-FOOLISH

During the 1960s, millions of Americans set off to see the world on the cheap by backpacking, staying in hostels and cheap hotels, camping out in parks, or sleeping on cathedral steps. I was one of the pilgrims.

We all bought pamphlets and books that told us how to travel cheaply. Quality was a secondary concern. In one of the books there was a description of a way to get from Paris to the palace at Versailles for just a few francs. The plan involved taking trains and commuter buses instead of going directly on a tour bus from downtown Paris.

I tried it. Instead of enjoying the palace, I spent hours getting off one train, waiting for another, looking for bus stops. The buses were usually late, and once I got on the wrong one. Finally, exhausted and frustrated, I arrived at my destination. I had saved a few francs, but I had wasted the better part of one of my few days in France. It was a false economy.

Travelers still do this sort of thing. I observed the pattern in Las Vegas recently. This gambling mecca is noted for its inexpensive food. The casinos are more than willing to subsidize the meals just to attract and keep people in the building.

The problem with the giveaway food prices is the long lines. At one casino, I observed a 100-yard-long line of people waiting in line for as long as an hour just to purchase a $3.99 buffet breakfast. Fifty feet away, they could have been seated immediately at a restaurant that charged only $3.00 more per person. The people in line, who wouldn't spend three dollars more for breakfast, hurried back to the casinos after breakfast, where they risked many times the $3.00 on one game of chance.

The rule time tacticians follow is: Don't allow cost to be your only criterion.

There are numerous instances of being penny-wise, hours-foolish. If you choose the airport shuttle bus instead of a cab, you may lose valuable time waiting for the shuttle to arrive and waiting for it to fill up with riders, and then spending more valuable time as it drops off passengers one by one at the various hotels along the way. Often, for just a few dollars more, you can leave immediately in a cab and go directly to your destination. In fact, the cab drive may cost you less than the shuttle if you find someone to share the ride.

Other examples: Living far away from your work just to save money (a topic discussed earlier) is a variation of this principle. If your office has an antiquated copying machine, and people have to stand in line to get their copying done, it's costing you money to keep it. Don't hold on to any slow, inefficient, antiquated technology when reliable and faster technology is available. Many organizations keep repairing old computers and old copying machines, even though the new ones are of much higher quality, faster, and easier to use. They choose to remain saddled with slow, anemic technology.

When you attend meetings and conventions, staying at a small motel in the suburbs instead of booking a room in your convention hotel can be penny-wise and hours-foolish. If a meeting is worth going to, it's probably worth making the extra investment to be where the action is, to be where you can rub shoulders with key players in the organization and increase the likelihood that serendipitous encounters with people who can help you will occur.

Don't spend valuable time driving back and forth to the sessions instead of networking or attending important formal or informal sessions; the move may turn out not to be very career-efficient. Moreover, by staying off-site, you may be advertising that you are not a player.

I learned an important lesson years ago on my way between Paris and Versailles. If there's any way to do it, I try to use fast technology, catch a taxi instead of waiting forever at lonely bus stops, paying the going rate instead of always pinching a penny. It's a lot quicker and often less expensive in the long run.

❧

THE USE AND ABUSE OF MEETINGS: TO MEET OR NOT TO MEET

"I spend all day in meetings," a manager in a major corporation complained recently. "I have to stay late, come in early, or work on weekends just to keep up with the regular flow of work, plus develop all the ideas that people think of in the nonstop meetings." No name need be associated with this lament, because it's a cliché in many organizations,

A meeting has the potential of serving several functions. Here are the main ones:

- *Communication.* A group is called together to announce a dividend hike or the appointment of a new director.

- *Problem solving.* A group works together to brainstorm in order to find a solution to a problem.

- *Crisis management and damage control.* A group meets to deal with false rumors that are spreading and could cause conflict.

- *Status reinforcement.* A group meets, with the president regularly seated in the president's chair and the directors in chairs at the head table. This is a ritual that reinforces the perception that these individuals are special.

- *Emotional support.* A group meets to recognize the award-winning performance of a member.

Because of the multiple functions that a meeting can serve, it is too simple to say: "Don't call a meeting. Just send a memo." The person calling the meeting may have more in mind than just communication. Attending meetings may not be separate from "doing your work." In many occupations, it is your work. If that mode of activity doesn't suit your personality, you may want to consider another field or another job in the same field.

If you are charged with the responsibility to call a meeting, here are some guidelines to follow:

- If all you want to do is communicate information, you need not call a meeting. Unless there is a strong need to have questions and answers in a group setting, a memo or electronic mail will be more effective. The advantage of the meeting is that at least you know who is in the room when the information was shared, and you can evaluate verbal and nonverbal responses.

- If the meeting is primarily for problem solving, you may be able to jump-start the meeting by using an advance memo or electronic mail to announce the general topic to be discussed and provide background data so that participants can begin thinking about solutions. You might ask participants to come prepared with material on the subject. Meeting face-to-face provides the opportunity for happy accidents to occur. Participants might not think of a solution unless they hear the comments of other participants.

   A promising new development for problem solving is a computer technology called groupware. Participants type into computers their solutions and reactions prior to the meeting or as the meeting is taking place. They can read in real time what other participants are saying, and can evaluate and rank those reactions quickly. Because ideas need not be associated with names, groupware enables the ideas of less aggressive and lower-status members to be looked at and evaluated.

- If there's a crisis, call a meeting of key players, or at least contact them by phone or electronic mail. They will want to get their ideas heard, and you will be blamed if you don't give them a chance. The same people who gripe about too many meetings will criticize leaders who never call meetings, complaining that they are autocratic and don't involve them in decisions.

- Leaders need rituals to enhance and preserve their status. If you are a meeting planner, the ritual is a way of reinforcing the structure of the organization. But you don't want to overdo this. A poorly attended meeting designed for leadership status enhancement is worse than no meeting at all.

- If you can make the meeting enjoyable, the other functions will be easier to attain.

- Begin on time. Don't punish those who arrive on time by making them wait for those who don't. There will be some exceptions, like making sure that someone who's strategic to a project is present, or waiting for a guest presenter who is detained. But these are clearly exceptions.

- Start with soft and easy items first and then move to the tougher, more time-consuming items. (See "Exceptions to the Jackie Ward Rule" in Chapter 8.)

- Keep on track. A printed agenda will help.

- Pay attention to timing and pacing. Striking a balance between a tense, compulsive, time-driven meeting and a soft, fuzzy, time-waster is not easy. A mix of serious and light items is often desirable. A joke or humorous story, even badly told, can help relieve tension or boredom.

- When you're finished, quit. This is especially true of regular meetings, like the weekly sales meeting. Adjourn the meeting when you've covered everything. Then those who want to hang around and chat may do so and people who need to get to other things may leave.

- Practice. Conducting a meeting well is science and art. Only after long experience, with good feedback, will you develop a feel for how to pace the meeting. Many masters of this craft perfected their skills in college organizations, like clubs or sororities/fraternities. If your school days are just a memory, you can still hone your skills in volunteer, civic, and religious organizations, and especially in Toastmasters.

DEVELOP SURVIVAL SKILLS IF YOU'RE ABSENTMINDED

Millions of work hours are lost every day by people looking for things: managers looking for misplaced reports and letters; researchers looking for misplaced books, monographs and quotes; administrators looking for misplaced invoices and receipts. Even though this is a common ailment, society does precious little to help the absentminded. Time management books rarely mention how to cope with the malady.

Fortunately many absentminded people make important contributions to society. But they go into tailspins regularly, spending hours looking for misplaced articles. Invaluable time is lost retracing steps, asking everyone along the trail: Have you seen the report? my book? my glasses? my keys? my papers? The emotional stress that accompanies these episodes can range from mild discomfort to catatonic seizures.

Some time ago my life screeched to a traumatic stop for several unpleasant hours. I misplaced my appointment book. That may not seem like much of a problem to people who do not live by their appointments, but for those of us who do, it is nothing short of a calamity. During that time, no plans could be made, no invitations accepted, nothing constructive could be done. I was totally distracted. Someone called to see if I could do a keynote speech for their organization. I wanted to do it very much, but I didn't know whether I was already booked or not. I didn't know what I had agreed to do at nine o'clock the next morning, let alone at nine o'clock two months from then.

I retraced my steps, phoning everyone along the way, describing the book, asking them please to call me if anyone turned it in. I imagined all the places I could have put it down and looked several times even where I could not possibly have placed it.

After looking frantically, calling everyone, I finally acquiesced to fate. Perhaps someone would find it and call. I decided to take a nap, because I was mentally and emotionally exhausted. I would wait for the phone to ring. After all, I had put my name and address in the book. Please ring, phone. Dear God, let it ring.

After a few minutes in the prone position, I resolved to look in my car for the fourth time, and there I found the blessed book, hiding in a little nook between the seat and the door.

My life began again. That day, I decided to take immediate steps to protect me in the future. I developed a survival plan for the absentminded. Here are the main features of the plan:

■ *A place for everything and everything in its place.* Select a spot to put your glasses, your favorite pen, your keys, and your appointment book, and discipline yourself to return them to that spot every time. Create a rational arrangement for your files, books, and reports, and then faithfully put them back in their place. Carry items in the same part of your clothing, for example, the billfold always in one pocket, glasses in another. This small discipline not only serves as a prevention against loss, but it also means that you can carry out certain tasks on auto-pilot without having to devote a great deal of brain power to the task. You reach for your billfold, glasses, or business cards automatically.

Train yourself not to deviate from the plan. When you deviate, use negative reinforcement. Do something to yourself that is painful.

You should rationally and intelligently choose the spot for the object, not select some difficult-to-remember or difficult-to-use place. You might even select two alternate places, like either the nightstand or your desk for your glasses. Abraham Lincoln is said to have had a file in his law office labeled: "If nowhere else, look for it here."

- *Don't hide things.* You may be so clever that you'll forget where you hid them. My mother spent her entire adult life hiding valuables from a thief who never came. An object that is lost is just as effectively gone as one that is stolen.

- *Enlist the aid of a patient,* presentminded *(as opposed to absentminded) friend.* Tell that person where you're putting your files, folders, books, and the like. But don't select someone who will belittle you or become cross with you because of your affliction. And never choose an absentminded person for this assignment. If the absentminded leads the absentminded, they shall both lose their minds.

- *Write your name, address, and phone number on valuable items. And offer a reward.* Sometimes this works. If you lose something and a finder returns it, don't be cheap. Pay the reward cheerfully. Time management consultant Harold Taylor recommends keeping working papers in a large, self-addressed envelope instead of a folder in case you leave it on the plane or in the hotel. If you do, you'll have a better chance of having it returned.

- *Label files and folders carefully.* Cryptically labeled files and folders are easily lost, especially if those files and folders are in a computer with a long menu.

- *Be redundant.* Whenever possible, create two of everything. Create two identical files with different names. This is easy to do with a photocopier. Computer files can be readily copied and given different names.

- *Look before you leap.* This is an old adage, like "a place for everything and everything in its place." But I have found that most of what I have lost in my life was lost when I was leaping. I left a wonderful camera on a seat in a waiting area in Honolulu's airport when I hurried off to catch a plane. When I realized what I had done and rushed back, it wasn't there. I have lost valuable materials in the computer when someone interrupted me or I rushed off to a meeting, and did not take time to save before leaping into a conversation or going to a meeting. If you have to leave anywhere in a big hurry, discipline yourself to look before you do. Every airline in the world has rooms bulging with unclaimed items, many of them expensive and some irreplaceable, left behind by people leaping.

- *Use cues and reminders.* When you park in a large parking lot, make a notation of what row and level you are on, and take the note with you. There are numerous situations in which a written note or some kind of cue can jog your memory. Sometimes, you won't have to actually write it down. If you think you'll forget something, leave the reminder on your voice mail or answering machine. This is especially helpful if you have a car phone and an idea that you think you might forget occurs to you while driving.

My anguish over misplacing an appointment book long ago was so great, I decided to make a list of everything which, if lost, could bring all activity to a stop. I made a duplicate or backup of all these items and gave them to my daughter, who happens to be presentminded and patient. Now she has backup diskettes of essential files, my passport number, and an extra set of keys. I bought an extra set of glasses. If I lose them—and I will eventually—I can order a new pair and use the spare until the replacement arrives.

What about my appointment book? I now have two. One stays at my desk. The other is a portable computer. I update both each day. The extra time I spend being redundant is better than the alternative.

❧ 10 ❧

Don't Let Others Waste Your Time

LEARN TO RECOGNIZE AND AVOID TIME THIEVES

Scott Adams has drawn a wonderful *Dilbert* cartoon that shows Dilbert hard at work composing his new business management book. One chapter of Dilbert's book is entitled "Time Management." His first piece of advice is, "Always postpone meetings with time-wasting morons." A moronish-looking character standing behind him asks: "How do you do that?" Dilbert replies, "Can I get back to you on that?"

Highly successful people postpone meetings with time-wasters or avoid them altogether. "I am always punctual because my time is important and the other guy's time is important," Stanley Marcus once told me. "If I find that people aren't going to reciprocate, then I find a way of doing business with somebody else."

That principle is followed by top people in many fields. One of Minolta's best salespeople told me, "The really good salespeople in this company won't let people keep them waiting around."

Unfortunately, there are situations in which you are hostage to other people's agendas. You may be a sales rep, sitting in the waiting room for a buyer who's inside the office and doesn't care if you go away. If the person inside is absolutely crucial to you, there's not a lot you can do except to wait and adopt defensive time tactics—like reading a paperback or report that you brought with you or making a few calls if a phone is available outside of earshot of the receptionist.

If you have ongoing interaction between a person who has more power than you, you may be able to work out an arrangement with that person's gatekeeper. (Surprisingly, many salespeople, vendors, and other individuals who need to get through don't bother to cultivate these people.)

Through the years, I have had to deal with a president of a television network and later the president of a university, both of whom often ran behind schedule and kept people waiting for long periods of time. By getting to know their executive secretaries, I was able to minimize the wait time by calling beforehand and getting a reading on how their schedules were going. Sometimes, if they were running very late, their secretaries would call a few minutes before the time they felt I would actually get in.

There are some proactive measures you may be able to take. A sales manager told me: "I won't let a doctor or dentist keep me waiting long. I'll wait 15 minutes. Then I go to the receptionist and say, 'Is the doctor ready to see me? My appointment was for three o'clock. If he can't, I'll have to reschedule, *because I have pending appointments....*' And you know what? They'll usually take you."

A college administrator told me that one of her colleagues takes innumerable phone calls during their meetings. If the interruptions become excessive, she writes a note and passes it to him: "I can see you're busy. Please call me when you're free." Then she gets up and leaves.

Sometimes it's a relative or a good friend who steals your time. They wouldn't think of being late for a business appointment, but they take a time-robbing approach with you. What to do?

With some people, you can just discuss it frankly. If it's an ongoing problem, wait until the next occasion when you set a time to meet. When the time to meet is being agreed upon, say something like, "Do you think we can meet *right at 4:00* (or, perhaps make it even more precise, like "right at 4:10?") I'm juggling several errands and projects and if I get behind, I'll be in real trouble."

If talk doesn't work, borrow a few pages from the ideas of B. F. Skinner. Skinner advised waiting until you catch the other person doing what you want—like showing up precisely on time—and then positively reinforcing him or her. The reinforcement might be no more than warm words of recognition, such as, "I really appreciate your showing up so punctually." Sincere appreciation often can get you a lot more of what you want.

One final defensive measure against the time thieves. Control the site of meetings. If you are at your office or home, and they don't show or are late, you are in a place where you can continue to do some other task. With drop-in visitors, whose qualities are not known, one executive I know meets in the waiting room instead of taking them to his office. It's easier to break off the meeting in the reception area than it is in your office.

❧
DON'T ADOPT OTHER PEOPLE'S MONKEYS

Don't put that monkey on my back. —TRADITIONAL SAYING

If you value your time, you must be careful when you're around people with pet monkeys. First thing you know, they'll want to put one on your back.

Better be careful. Taking care of monkeys can be very time consuming. Some monkeys can be delightful little creatures, but they also can be bad-mannered, nasty, and tiresome.

Don't take on every problem or responsibility (i.e., monkey) that other people want to give you. If you accept every problem that's proffered you, your life can become a nightmare. Many a manager has spent days, months, even years dealing with monkeys that jumped from their rightful owners onto their own back.

Avoiding other people's rightful responsibility is the thesis of a book entitled *The One Minute Manager Meets the Monkey*.[31] The authors—Kenneth Blanchard, William Oncken, Jr., and Hal Burrows—tell horror stories about managers who spend every waking hour trying to deal with monkeys that they permitted to jump from their owner's backs onto their own. These managers have become supervised by their subordinates, who stop by their offices each morning to inquire about how the manager is coming along with their problems. In a ridiculous turnabout, the subordinates are delegating tasks to the managers instead of being delegated to. Sometimes, the manager doesn't even realize this.

After reading *The One Minute Manager Meets the Monkey*, a corporation president who attended one of my time management workshops, shared the book with several key people in the organization. The idea of the monkey became a part of their corporate culture. Today, the employees make little jokes about their monkeys. Sometimes, an employee will come up to an associate and say, "I have this monkey on my back that's getting too much for me. Can you give me a little help?" They joke about the monkey, but they understand the principle.

Recently, I consulted with the president of a company in the communications industry. He was having problems getting his work done. Why? His people came to him every time there was a crisis, even minor ones. They expected him to solve all their problems.

When I mentioned the monkey principle to him, a light clicked on. He realized how crazy his system had become. He was literally working for the people who were supposed to be working for him. I saw him a few weeks later, after he had taken steps to let people solve their own problems. He was more upbeat than I had ever seen him. He had managed to get control over his work again.

If you are monkey-ridden, here are three rules Blanchard, Oncken, and Burrows recommend:

- Remember that the world is full of monkeys, so pick only a monkey that you really care about.

- Make people care for their own monkeys. You shouldn't try to solve other people's problems if they aren't willing to do anything about it themselves. There's nothing wrong with giving them a hand with their monkeys now and then just as long as you make sure they keep their monkeys after you've finished helping.

- If you're a manager, assign monkeys to capable people in your organization. Coach them on their new responsibilities. If you're a manager, you should measure your success by what you are able to get your people to do.

Experts on monkey management say that there will always be more monkeys clamoring for our attention than you will have time to manage. If you let every monkey on your back, it's bad for you and bad for the monkeys.

Accepting the wrong monkeys can mean that the right monkeys will languish for lack of attention. But if you can persuade others to keep their own monkeys and give them the proper care and attention they deserve, the monkeys may turn out to be well-loved pets, not pests, that will bring those people joy and perhaps recognition.[32]

One of the best practitioners of this management approach is Gene Roberts, former executive editor of *The Philadelphia Enquirer*. During the 18 years Roberts was with the paper, it garnered an astonishing 17 Pulitzer prizes. Clearly, Roberts didn't do all the writing or shoot all the photographs himself. He did it through others. One of his favorite techniques was to keep his people's monkeys off his back.

Roberts's colleagues remember his long trancelike silences during meetings with them. His silence had the effect of forcing others to talk. "He once told me," said one of his former colleagues, Bill Kovach, "that one of the most important lessons I would ever learn about managing people...was that most people will solve their own problems and give you a solution if you only listen to them, if you keep them talking long enough."[33]

After a workshop in New Jersey two years ago, Louis Tischler, the amiable president of Westwood Computer Corporation, invited me into his office. As we entered, I saw a sign over the entrance:

DON'T BRING ME PROBLEMS
BRING ME SOLUTIONS

I like Tischler's approach, with one caveat. If you're a manager, you want your people to feel comfortable telling you about some of their problems. Many a company got into big trouble because people were afraid to let management know bad news. I recommend encouraging your people to feel comfortable telling bad news, but always with a suggested solution.

ॐ

JUST SAY NO

When I asked TV superstar Larry King what time-wasters he tried most to avoid, he replied without hesitation: "Boring lunches... being with people I don't want to be with." Then he added, "I find that the more you obtain in life, professionally and financially, you can pick and choose that better. I don't have that lunch that I have to go to."

Unless it's a command performance, time tacticians try to avoid meetings, appointments, and social events that they know will be a waste of time. If they are a part of a regular routine that they're obligated to attend, there may be no way to escape them. Then they endure them, focusing on ways to improve them, and sending a substitute as often as they can get away with it.

If you're asked by a friend to take on a project, but you're over-loaded or you don't have any real interest in the project, here's a response that a lot of good time tacticians use: "I'm sorry, but I won't be able to help you with that *at this time.*"

I have in my possession a letter written from one corporation president to another. One has asked the other to help him raise money for a philanthropy that they both know about. Listen to the elegant way one president turns down the other:

> I appreciate your invitation to get actively involved in this new solicitation on behalf of_____. Unfortunately, I have only so much time available and there are so many worth-while projects, I don't feel that I can take on another one just now. It would be a disservice to us both since I doubt that I would be able to give your project the attention it deserves.

If diplomacy is a requirement for the job that he holds, you can see why he was chosen.

Here's a rejection note that I once received. Observe that it has essentially the same elements as the one previously quoted:

> Unfortunately, I am going to have to put your proposal on hold for right now. We simply have too much on our plates to continue discussions with you at the present time. However, I

will keep your information in our "active" file, should the situation change.

But the best rejection letter I have ever seen was written by the editor of an Asian publishing house to an aspiring author:

> We have read your manuscript with boundless delight. If we were to publish your book, it would be impossible for us to ever again publish any work of a lower order. And as it is unthinkable that, in the next 1000 years, we shall see its equal, we are, to our profound regret, compelled to return your divine composition, and beg you a thousand times to overlook our short sight and timidity.

Sometimes you may have to say no to the person that you report to. How should you do that? Very carefully. Keep in mind that a good manager will want to know when you can't possibly do all that you've been asked to do. One effective tactic is to express concern about having to neglect something else that they want done. Couch your comments in terms of priorities. Saying something like the following may work: "I'm working on the report you and I talked about. I'm concerned that if I put off doing the report to go to the three o'clock meeting, I might not get it finished on time. I'm quite willing to go to the meeting. Which do you prefer?"

MAKE YOURSELF SCARCE

Sometimes it's smart to be hard to find. Retreats and hideaways serve this purpose beautifully. Having more than one office works well, too.

Some time tacticians achieve this goal by telling intruders to go away. For example, a person working on deadline posted this note on the door:

> Anyone Who Interrupts Me Before 4:00 Will Be Cheerily Welcomed. NOT.

All of us are invited to events that we don't want to attend, by people we aren't particularly interested in spending time with. The simplest way to deal with these situations is to say, "I'd really love to do that, but I won't be able to go that evening," or "Thank you for asking me, but I have a conflict."

Some successful individuals recommend offering no explanation whatever. Never explain, they advise. The less you explain, the better. Your friends won't expect it and your enemies won't believe it.

However, most people have to resort to diplomatic ways to say no. The well-tested ones are health problems, "conflicts," car problems, and prior commitments. Some of these are included in the next section.

EXPAND YOUR TIME-CUE VOCABULARY

In television and radio, there are two well-known cues that are used to indicate that time is running out. Floor managers will rotate their hands in a clocklike manner. This means to speed up. The other is the sign of the slashed throat. It means, "Cut. Stop immediately. Time has expired."

Often in everyday life, you will need to give people you're talking to cues about how much time you have. Some individuals have no difficulty whatsoever saying, "I've got to run. See you," and simply hang up or get up and leave.

Ted Turner is like that. Once I needed to see him just before the holidays. He told me at the outset of our conversation that he was very busy but that he would give me five minutes. I presented my idea as rapidly as possible, but ran over by a few seconds. When I paused for the next sentence, Turner interrupted: "Your five minutes are up. I love you, professor, but I gotta go. Merry Christmas." Then he arose from his chair, walked toward his desk, and began working through his papers. The meeting was over.

We've all been in situations when we needed to be somewhere else very soon, yet there seemed to be no way to extract ourselves from the present conversation without offending the person talking. Meanwhile, the old stomach churned while we waited for that person to reach a stopping point.

The alternative to abrupt terminations is to learn to use time cues. If you use them, you'll be more in control of your agenda and you'll earn the respect and appreciation of most of the people who deal with you.

Let people know what you expect. If you want to let people know that six-thirty means six-thirty, you can say, "I don't think we can leave a minute later than six-thirty because traffic will be heavy," and let them know you'll leave then.

If punctuality is not critical, that can be indicated by the wonderful suffix *-ish,* as in "The party will begin at seven*ish.*" If *ish* isn't used in your circle of acquaintances, say *"about* seven." (In Latin America, it's considered fashionable to be late to a social event and impolite to show up precisely at the stated time. If you're expected to be punctual, some South Americans will say "American time.") I know of one executive who schedules his appointments at, say, 10:05 or 4:35 or 3:40 rather than on the hour or the quarter or the half. It's his way of signaling that his appointment schedule is precise.

When you confirm an appointment, you can use a time cue. For example, "Hi, I'm Sharon. I'm on a real tight schedule today, and just wanted to check to see if everything's still on." Giving the cue—"I'm on a really tight schedule today"—can be very effective. The confirmation tells you that the person you want to see is there. The cue tells the person you're calling that time is important to you.

There will always be some individuals who won't pick up on cues. Nothing will work for them except unequivocal terminations. USA Network chief Kay Koplovitz has an open-door policy for employees. However, when she feels the meeting should end, she will turn and begin to work on papers on her credenza behind her desk. "I try to wind up the conversation as I'm turning around, not to be rude, but I do. You have to sometimes," Koplovitz told me. "And you have to push your chair back and get up and escort people to the door sometimes. I find that's a time saver."

Learning how to use a few simple cues will save a few minutes here and there. A strong repertoire, used well, can reduce your stress level plus enhance your reputation for being socially skillful and courteous.

Here are some of the most effective ones:

- *The time-frame cue.*   This signal is given *at the start* of the interaction. Ted Turner used a variation of the time-frame cue in the meeting I just described. This cue can sound something like this: "You caught me in-between meetings, so I have only about four or five minutes to spare." If you like, you can continue with a comment like, "I really want to talk with you. We can get started now, if you like. If we don't cover all that we need to, we'll reschedule a time when we won't have to rush. Is that okay?"

  Some time tacticians control expectations by announcing at the beginning of a meeting something like: "Let me tell you now that I will need to make an important phone call at four o'clock." It's important to announce this at the beginning, not at five minutes till four. Seminar leader Bill Johnson often begins an outgoing call this way: "Hi, Ed. This is Bill. Do you have time for a couple of quick questions?" Johnson says this approach is friendly, yet it quickly conveys the message that you are not in a chit-chat mood. Johnson sometimes will interrupt *himself* in the middle of a sentence if he feels the call is going too long. Johnson will say something like: "I'm sorry, Martha. I just noticed the time. Were there any other items we need to cover?"

  This time-frame cue has three purposes: (1) It indicates to other people that they are important to you, that you really want to spend time with them and hear what they have to say. (2) It provides the other people with parameters so that they know in advance how much time you can give them. (3) It forces the other party to get to the heart of the matter and not waste time with irrelevant details.

  Sometimes people need to talk about a subject that cannot be adequately discussed in the time that you can give them at that moment. If that's the case, set another time. Some individuals will never divulge really vital information if they feel rushed.

- *Nonverbal cues.* You can begin to stack material together as though you are getting ready to leave the office. You can lean forward in your chair, or begin to get papers together as though you are about to leave. The most obvious nonverbal cue is to stand up.

- *Pauses and silence.* Create longer and longer silences between comments.

- *The speed-up cue.* Here's an example of how you can use it in an interaction, especially if the conversation is on the phone: "I know you're busy, but I have a quick question." Intimating that the other party is busy is a polite way of saying, "I'm busy." What it does is set up a quick-step rhythm for the interaction. Here's another: "Kim, before I have to take my next appointment, I need to ask you..." or, "Before we hang up, I want to be clear on one point." Or, "Kim, I'm supposed to be at a meeting that started five minutes ago, but I don't want to rush our conversation. When can I get back to you?"

- *The staged interruption.* Some executives have their assistants interrupt after a certain amount of time has elapsed. The assistants announce quietly that the next appointment has arrived or remind the executives that they need to leave soon for their next meeting.

- *The "looking for something" gambit.* I have seen time tacticians pay complete attention to the other person for a while, but after a certain amount of time has elapsed, they would start looking for something on their desk or elsewhere in the office. They would appear to be somewhat distracted and even slightly apologetic. Visitors get the not-too-subtle message that they have received about all the total attention they are going to receive, and bring the meeting to a conclusion. This gambit is one of Ted Turner's favorites.

- *Props.* Karen E. Shepherd, who represents a book publisher on college campuses, keeps a timer in her purse that goes off after 10 minutes have elapsed. She then announces that she needs to go to her next appointment or make a phone call. If she feels the conversation needs to continue, she simply cuts off the alarm.

- *The close.* Some people have great difficulty ending a conversation. They will say "good-bye" several times, each one in a slightly different manner. There are ways to close quickly and politely. Here's one of the most effective ones I've encountered. Management consultant Roger E. Herman once used it on me. I liked it so much that I wrote it down and have used it myself occasionally. Here's the way he wrapped up the conversation: "Well, Gene, I'll get back to you soon. (Pause) Thanks a lot." And he was gone.

One place where you need to know how to extricate yourself is at stand-up events, like receptions and parties. You may not want to spend all your time with one individual. What to do? Socially adept individuals will greet you cordially, and all the time they are with you will focus on you. Then, they will say something like, "I've really enjoyed chatting with you but I need to talk with some other people before they leave." Other versions: "I'd better start circulating and meet everyone," or "Can we talk later? I need to speak to some other people before they leave." Then smile and move on.

THE HIGH COST OF A FREE MEAL

When I was an impoverished college student, I eagerly accepted invitations to events that provided free food or drinks. In order to eat, I found myself attending speeches, presentations, political rallies, religious services, and parties given by people I barely knew. But I soon learned that I had to resist sales pitches, endure speeches I had no interest in, and participate in activities that I would surely have avoided if I had not been tempted by the freebies. Gradually, I concluded that most freebies aren't worth the price you pay for them.

One great American pastime involves trying to get something for nothing or at a deep discount. It's a trap. Avoid it. Don't spend your life trying to get people to do things for you for nothing. You may be successful from time to time, but generally when someone does something for you as a favor, you lose control over the quality of the product or the timeliness with which it is delivered.

How can you complain if something is done shabbily if you didn't pay for it? An old proverb puts it this way: "Don't look a gift horse in the mouth." If you didn't pay anything for the horse, it's bad form to examine its teeth. If it's done for you for free, you generally have to take what you get.

It's not just quality that you lose control over. It's time. If somebody does something for you for nothing, they often give it low priority. They will get to it when they can. Why should they put your work ahead of the work of paying customers? And why should you expect them to? Even a discount can weaken your ability to demand top quality and prompt service if other people are paying full price.

The solution is to pay top dollar for what you need. That way you can expect your work to be put at the front of the line and you can demand top quality. I know this advice runs counter to the belief that you should always seek the lowest price and try to get it free if you can. Here's what can happen if you live by that philosophy. A nationally known professional speaker has a big box full of defective cassettes because he tried to get something for nothing. He persuaded a friend to donate a "master" for the audiocassette that he needed to duplicate. Unbeknownst to him, the friend reversed the sides of the cassette. Without listening to the master, the speaker sent it to the duplicating facility. Two weeks later he received a big box containing 500 audiocassettes— with side "B" recorded on side "A." His friend didn't charge him for the work. But the speaker did have to pay for duplicating 500 cassettes that he could not use. This individual tried to get a free lunch but, as it turned out, he had to "eat" a box of 500 useless audiocassettes. And he had to start all over with a new order. This time he paid full price for the master. The speaker never told his friend who had made the mistake. "Why should I make my friend feel bad?" he explained. "He did it for nothing. Why waste more time telling him?"

Whenever I am tempted to try to get a free meal, I think about the speaker and his box of defective audiocassettes. Free meals are never free.

ॐ
THINK LIKE A POLITICIAN

Man is a political animal. —ARISTOTLE

Don't think that politics is something that takes place only at the courthouse, the state capital, or Washington. If people call you a politician, chances are they are not paying you a compliment. The word smacks of falseness, back slapping, and back-room deals. But the basic idea of politics is getting things done with people. In a way, politics is human engineering.

Some people feel that they don't need political or promotional skills. All they need is to do a good job or produce a fine product and recognition and rewards will automatically follow. That is not usually the case. Being good at what you do is not good enough. Every project has a political side to it. Neglect it and the project will move slowly or die.

Even if you don't think of yourself as a politician, you will have to deal with people who do. So, it's useful to know how they think, how they set their priorities. How does a seasoned politician decide which phone call to take, which person to see? The answer? Power. If politicians are confronted by a pile of phone messages waiting to be returned, the question is not, "Which call came in first?" Politicians ask, "Who in that pile of telephone messages is the most powerful? Who can help me? Who can hurt me?"

Mayors, senators, and top administrators receive letters and phone calls by the score, sometimes by the tens of thousands. If they answered every one personally, all they would ever do is talk on the telephone and dictate letters. So, most of the work is delegated. But even the delegated messages are dealt with on the same basis: Who is the most powerful? Who can help? Who can hurt?

Even individuals far from elected political office have to be sensitive to these kinds of concerns. I asked Mary D. Poole, former national president of the Junior League and now Vice President for Human Resources at Presbyterian Healthcare

Services in Albuquerque, which phone messages she answered first. Poole replied: "Messages from my board members and messages from donors." That's an obvious priority for someone in her position. Board members, who hire, fire, and give raises, and donors, who can make her look good if they're kept happy, get first priority.

If you know that this is the way top people deal with competing demands for their time, you'll understand why your call may not get answered immediately, if at all. If you're having trouble getting through, chances are that the person you're trying to get to or his or her gatekeeper doesn't think you can help or hurt very much.

All phone calls and all letters don't deserve equal treatment. Certainly you should give high priority to those people who can help you, those who can hurt you. Those who wish to survive must make sure that important messages get through, that important people get heard.

But the tactic has a dangerous downside. If assistants are told to put through only powerful people, they may not know who all the powerful people are. They may accidentally treat someone who's powerful like a nobody. Moreover, whenever people in high places listen only to the powerful, they miss important messages little people can give them.

❧ 11 ❧

Enlist Others to Save You Time

❧

BECOME A SQUEAKY WHEEL

The squeaky wheel gets the grease. —TRADITIONAL SAYING

How to get the grease.
Unfortunately, people who patiently accept slow service and poor quality tend to get more of the same. Their requests and orders get pushed behind those of people who are more insistent on quality. Why does this happen? It's not very difficult to figure out. When vendors and suppliers have to make a choice between finishing a job for a customer who's nice or one who's demanding, what often happens? Work for demanding customers gets done first and work for the nice guy slides. Vendors may even hate doing it, and hate the person they are doing it for, but they still do it. They do it to avoid unpleasantness. Avoidance of pain can be a powerful motivator.

But it doesn't have to be that way. Being nice doesn't mean that you have to sit back and let others crowd in front of you while you get the leftovers. There are ways to be nice and not finish last. One way is to learn how to complain effectively. Here are six rules that time tacticians follow:

1. *Try to deal with people and companies that care about their reputations.* If you do this, you won't need to complain very much

because they will take steps to see that your need to complain is minimized. If there is a problem, these kinds of people and companies will listen to you and often throw in something extra just to keep you happy.

2. *Be certain that you are on solid ground before you make a complaint.* Ask for information. You may find that you are misinformed or just plain wrong. If you lambaste someone, and then find out that they were in the right, you'll look foolish, and your credibility will be damaged. It's generally a good idea to start out gently, even if you are in the right. If you come on too strong, you just might turn someone into an enemy who could be a friend.

3. *Don't complain to just anybody.* Complain only to someone who can do something about your complaint. The only reason to ever complain to someone without discretionary authority is to vent your emotions. And there are better ways to do that than complaining to someone who's ineffectual.

   Go directly to the most important person available and have a quiet discussion. If this approach doesn't work, you can move your complaint up in intensity and up the hierarchy.

   Should you go to the very top at the very beginning? Sometimes. However, local managers and department heads usually are able to deal with run-of-the-mill problems satisfactorily.

4. *Remember that the way you complain is as critical as the person you complain to.* Begin with a compliment, if possible. If you are at a restaurant, you might begin by stating that you've eaten at the restaurant before (if you have) and enjoyed it immensely. If you haven't been there before, indicate that you came because of its excellent reputation. Give them something to live up to.

   Begin sympathetically. Remember that this individual may not be personally involved in the situation or even know about it. If you explode with anger at the beginning, you may trigger a hostile, defensive response.

5. *Keep a firm hand on your temper.* If the experience has cost you time and money, you are probably annoyed. The situation may have embarrassed you. But you must maintain self-control. There's nothing wrong with expressing your annoyance. In fact, a display of anger in some situations can be highly effective, but

you must not "lose it." If you do, you run the risk of discrediting yourself and losing the contest as well. It's certainly appropriate to state that you're upset, but remain in control of your emotions.

6. *Don't complain about everything.* I once accompanied a successful architect as he inspected a building under construction. He walked over to some carpenters who were installing a window, looked carefully at their work, then walked away. Later he commented: "What they were doing wasn't perfect. It was slightly off, and they knew I knew. But I didn't say anything. I gave them that one. I'll give up the little goofs to catch the big ones. It's kind of a game. If everything's a battle, you lose the war."

I once heard the same basic idea from the conductor Maxim Shostakovich. He said a conductor during a rehearsal has to be able to know which mistakes are accidents and which should be corrected on the spot. "If it's an accident, the musician often knows, and will go home and practice and correct it himself. All you have to do is look at him or her. If you stop for every mistake, you'll never get through rehearsal."

Not long ago, I heard a receptionist take a call from a customer. It was obvious from her response that the person on the line was very unhappy. She told the caller that she had every right to be upset, and urged her to complain to the highest level. "They need to know," the receptionist stated. Then she gave the caller the names and direct phone numbers of several company executives, including the CEO.

When she got off the line, I stated that I could not help overhearing the conversation and was impressed by the manner in which she had handled the complaint. The receptionist replied: "Boy, was she angry. But she had good reason to be. The woman she was complaining about is terrible. It's about time somebody complained about her. I wanted to make sure she did."

Complainers don't always deserve a bad name. Often they have made the world better. A skillfully executed, well-timed complaint sometimes can do wonders for the one who speaks and sometimes for the one who listens.

How to deal with squeaky wheels.

Many highly successful people and companies deliberately invite complaints. They want this kind of information. They view complaints as a resource to help them become more efficient, more effective.

You may not have thought about *receiving* complaints as a time tactic. But you should. Complaints that are on the mark can make you more effective, help you focus, save you time. Here are eight rules to follow when receiving a complaint:

1. *Look at a complaint as potentially valuable information.* Every year, organizations spend millions of dollars paying consultants and research teams to find out what customers, and potential customers, think about them. Whenever someone complains to you, you are getting such information free.

2. *Evaluate the complaint.* Analyze the complaint to see what core elements of information it contains. Sometimes a complaint is like a volcanic eruption. The mixture may contain several basic complaints, some important, some trivial. Ask yourself, "What is in this complaint that I can use?"

3. *Evaluate the complainer.* Does the person really know? Is she going off half-cocked? Is he emotionally overwrought? Obviously, all complaints and complainers are not created equal.

   Stanley Marcus says complainers helped make Neiman-Marcus become a great store. He said a tiny percentage of hard-to-please customers found fault with everything. These were among the store's most discriminating customers. But one reason they were so hard to please was because they were well-traveled individuals who had seen the best in the world, and could afford to pay for it if they liked it. Instead of ignoring these individuals or treating them as troublemakers, Marcus courted them, listened carefully to their complaints, and as a result raised the standards of his Dallas department store to world class. He discovered that if he pleased them, he pleased others too. Count yourself lucky if somebody who's world class takes the time to criticize you.

4. *Create some psychological distance between yourself and the complaint, especially if it's harsh.* This takes practice. If someone is letting you have it with both barrels, or even if they are telling you gently, it's not always easy to realize that what you are hearing is information that might be very valuable.

   Don't let criticism destroy your self-confidence. The ego is fragile. One of the most important differentiating characteristics between achievers and nonachievers is how they handle failure and criticism. Nonachievers say, "I'm a failure." Achievers say, "I did something that didn't work. I'll do it better next time."

5. *Encourage the complainer to be specific.* The first overgeneralized comment isn't usually the best that you can get. In fact, one of the best ways to get specific information *and* calm down an irate complainer is to ask the following question: "Would you mind if I wrote this down?" This simple question informs the complainer that you are paying attention to what he or she is saying and regard it as important enough to make notes.

6. *Ask, "What can I do to make this right?"* Don't volunteer to do anything before you ask this magic question. The complainer might not want as much as you are prepared to offer.

7. *Settle the complaint cheerfully.* If you deal with the individual in an unfriendly or grudging manner, you may just as well do nothing. Settle the complaint in such a way that you bind the customer, client, or friend to you—even if you have to say no. Make that person feel so good about the manner in which you did it that he or she will want to deal with you again.

8. *If there's nothing do-able in the complaint, shrug it off.* Thank the person for taking the time to let you know, and then get on with your life. There will always be a tiny percentage of people out there who won't like you, no matter how hard you try, how talented you may be, or how good your product is. Don't let those kinds of people get to you. Thank them for taking the time to tell you, and abide by your own knowledge and experience.

TO SAVE TIME, SMILE

A captivating smile is one of the greatest assets you can possess. It can help you move to the front of the line, gain access to privileged information, and get service after closing time.

People don't like to work with individuals whom they think will be unpleasant. Beth Wicke, a casting director for ABC, says she looks carefully at the way actors slate an audition tape to see if they give off friendly vibes. During the slate—the front end of the audition tape when actors tell who they are and who their agent is—a winning smile can help convince casting agents and directors that the person will be easy to work with. Other things being equal, they will pick the friendly actor.

Only people who are extraordinarily talented or rich get what they want without smiling, and a smile doesn't hurt even them. The Chinese have a proverb: A man without a smiling face must not open a shop.

But your smile must not look phony. Nothing turns people off like an insincere, frozen, prolonged smile. If in doubt about your smile, look in the mirror, or better, videotape yourself. You may be sincere and not look it.

A sincere smile at the appropriate time can soften up the defenses, helping you get what you want with a minimum of effort and time expended. So, recognize this resource and use it.

LEARN TO TIP EFFECTIVELY: THE GERARDO PRINCIPLE

Gerardo Zampaglione was Italy's Ambassador to Pakistan when I spent a year in that nation as a Fulbright Professor at the University of Islamabad. We became good friends. Gerardo was the author of several books, and had held a number of important posts in the Italian diplomatic corps. One art Gerardo mastered was the ability to get good service in places not known for their service. Gerardo not only functioned adequately, but seemed to thrive in such situations.

One of the projects I assigned myself that year was to see how Gerardo managed to get so much done and enjoy himself while he was doing it. One of his best tactics was to *tip in advance.* When Gerardo checked into a hotel, other guests might be complaining about the quality of the food, problems with their rooms, slow service, and the like. However, Gerardo managed to get wonderful rooms, receive the best and tastiest food the dining room was capable of preparing, and have care and attention lavished upon him.

He understood that one of the main reasons for the tip is embodied in the acronym TIP: *To Insure Promptness.* When Gerardo checked in, he gave a generous tip to the concierge, to the desk clerk, to the bellman, and to any maid he saw on his floor. Word was soon telegraphed to the entire staff that here was a man who would reward good treatment. The staff made an instant calculation. If there was a choice about who to serve first, or who was to get the best food or flowers or the most important table, they would give it to the person who had already shown what he would do. Why should they take a chance lavishing attention on someone who might leave them very little or even stiff them?

I have tried this principle myself a number of times since then, at home and abroad, and I can assure you that it works. For example, if I'm at a good restaurant and in a hurry, I will tell the person who seats me that I'm pressed for time and ask him if he can speed things up in the kitchen. Then I'll slip a bill into his hand. I repeat the same maneuver when the server comes.

Do this unobtrusively. If the tip in advance produces satisfactory results—and about 90 percent of the time it will—I leave an extra gratuity at the end of the meal.

What's amazing is that the advance tip doesn't have to be very large. I've seen sluggish service transformed by a single one-dollar bill—paid in advance. Generally the amount that you tip in advance should be determined by how pricey the hotel or restaurant is and how much you expect your total bill to be.

A variation of Gerardo's rule is to call ahead to a restaurant and make a special kind of reservation. Here's how: Tell the maître d', manager, or headwaiter that you will be coming to the restaurant with an important client, customer, or friend. Tell that person that you want a good table and attentive, prompt service. Also, importantly, tell him or her that you don't want to be presented with a check at the end of the meal. At the time you make your reservation, give them your credit card number and authorize the restaurant to add a generous gratuity to the bill.

Tip generously at any restaurant that you patronize regularly. If you tip just a bit more than average, the level and speed of service will almost always improve. The time tactician knows that a tip is an investment.

One caution. Often there's a thin line between a tip and a bribe. Be sure to stay on the ethical side of the line. This tactic is recommended for situations in which a gratuity is generally recognized as a part of the worker's compensation.

Q: Waiter, how long for a table?
A: Thirty minutes or ten dollars. Whichever comes first.

MASTER THE ART OF INTERRUPTING

Your parents told you not to interrupt. But they gave you bad advice. You may never be heard if you wait for some nonstop talkers to invite you to make a comment. These types of individuals pose a problem. A certain amount of assertive behavior is required or they will run over you.

I've observed for a long time that the people who get to the top in business, government, education, and the military are better than their peers at communicating. They often are particularly good at being able to break in and out of a conversation.

Not long ago, I was having breakfast with two corporation presidents. At one point in the conversation, one of the individuals wanted to make a point, and here's the adroit way he worded the interruption: "Excuse me for interrupting you—and don't

lose your train of thought—but I would like to suggest that...."
He then introduced a new topic without halting the flow of conversation. This skill is a powerful part of any executive's social repertoire.

Here are some suggestions management consultant Barbara Pagano uses for skillful interruptions:

- *Wait until they breathe.*   If you're confronted by nonstop talkers, wait until they breathe to jump in. When they do, be ready. Jump in. Hit it.

- *Call people by name.*   It's music to their ears. People like to hear their own name. Use this momentary distraction to get in with your point.

- *Use body language with your words.*   If your opener is that you have two points to make, get that hand up with two fingers. Use your hand in open gesture, while saying, "Let's look at another side of this...."

- *Touch the other person.*   Obviously, do this sparingly. If the nonstop talker is the opposite sex, you don't want to get into trouble for harassment. However, when you invade nonstop talkers' space, it can momentarily distract them so that you can get a word in.

- *Be sure you have something to say.*   If you interrupt and contribute nothing, you'll have trouble getting in the next time.

There's some scientific evidence which indicates that the ability to interrupt skillfully is a mark of high social intelligence. It can be learned and cultivated, but it often manifests itself very early in life. Kenneth Dodge, a psychologist at Duke University, has observed that youngsters who have little *social* intelligence, when they try to enter a game with other kids, will jump right in. "They're puzzled when they get rebuffed," he says. However, children with high social intelligence will enter a game step by step. They might make comments at first about the game or the group playing. Then they will ask if they might join the next game.

We normally think of interruptions taking place in conversations, but interruptions can be very effective in other contexts as well. For example, suppose you are standing in a long line to get a driver's license and you are not sure if you are standing in the right line. What should you do? You could stand patiently in line until you get to the counter and ask then. Or you could request the person behind you to hold your place while you go to the front of the line and ask: "May I ask a very quick question? Is this the line for....?" It's a simple and seemingly obvious maneuver, but many people don't avail themselves of it.

ENLIST THE AID OF COACHES

"We tell all our salespeople to find a coach" says Joan Mannis, a successful sales manager with the Octel Corporation. A "coach" is someone within a target organization who can assist in the sale.[34]

A coach may be able to tell you who the decision makers are, how to get to them, and how to stroke them. A coach can tell you how the project is going, whether competitors are coming in, and whether their ideas are being entertained. A coach can let you know about hidden agendas that you're not aware of, like changes in management, timetables for the project, budgetary restraints, and the like. Mannis says she's had coaches call to tell her the company was planning to sign a contract with a competitor the next day. That told her that she needed to get back for a last-minute push.

Coaches can be found or created at a number of places in an organization. They can be low-level people who attend key meetings. They are the ones who take notes or carry in the coffee. But they know what's going on. They can be receptionists, telephone operators, secretaries, administrative assistants, plus first-level or mid-level managers if you're selling a big-ticket item.

How do you recruit them? Suggest that you get together for lunch. When you do, begin to build a relationship. Find a mutual interest. Ask for advice. Most people love to give it.

Ask for help. Professional speaker and trainer Austin McGonigle believes one of the most powerful questions one person can ask is: "I wonder if you might help me?" He says it seldom fails to get a positive response. Most people basically want to be helpful. If they believe in you and the product or idea you're promoting, the potential for their becoming a coach is already there.

What's in it for the coach? One reward coaches receive is seeing someone they like get what they want. Also, they gain attention that they may not get anywhere else. "I've taken many a secretary to lunch," Mannis says. "You have to be careful that what you do isn't a bribe. It's not the amount of money that you spend on the lunch, anyway. How often does somebody take a secretary to lunch? I come by and pick them up and take them to a nice place."

How do you deal with a coach? Here's a typical conversation: "Hello, Gail. This is Joan. When I make my presentation tomorrow, who's going to be there? What are their positions? Would you say I should do a slide presentation?" If Gail tells you that the key decision maker hates slide presentations, you know what not to do.

Some professional salespeople recommend trying to have more than one coach. The reason is that a particular coach may lose his effectiveness as soon as the project moves to another unit. Once the project moves to the CEO's office, for example, he may no longer be able to track it.

This tactic is not just for people in outside sales. Most of the time most of us are selling something. As salespeople, we need the kind of information a coach can provide, whether we're selling a computer system, trying to get a bill passed by the legislature, or trying to get a job.

A young woman by the name of Sharon was employed as a salesperson but felt stifled in her job. Prospects for growth and advancement were virtually nonexistent in the company she worked for. Sharon was enrolled in an acting class which she hoped would help her with her communications skills in sales. Besides, the course was fun. At the class she discovered that one of her fellow students was in sales, too. They quickly became friends. Toward the end of the course, Sharon was told that the company her new friend worked for had an unexpected vacancy. Would she like to apply? "Of course," Sharon replied.

Because the job was an extremely attractive one, there were many applicants. As the list of candidates narrowed, Sharon received daily updates about what was happening from her friend. When she called back for a second interview, her coach told her what to say, what not to say. And when the choice was being made between two candidates, the coach put in a good word for Sharon. Guess who was chosen? Sharon, of course. If you want to save time and increase the likelihood of your success, find a coach.

ॐ

ASSOCIATE WITH TIME-CONSCIOUS PEOPLE AND COMPANIES

If time is valuable to you—and you wouldn't be reading this book if it weren't—it makes sense to look for people who value the same things that you do. This means that you will want to do business with people and companies that respect your time.

Many organizations clearly value their customers' time. They know that customers don't like to be kept waiting. So they work constantly at making sure that their operation is efficient. They spend lots of time thinking about how to make the system efficient, then evaluating it, and fine-tuning it. Federal Express, UPS, and Airborne Express are superb. So are Hertz and Avis. The way the Disney people handle throngs of people at its theme parks is the subject matter of books, articles, and case studies at business schools.

In choosing a product, service, or vendor, don't base your selection on price alone. If you save $20 a night on your hotel room, but you spend a lot of your time in line waiting to check in or waiting for a plumber to repair your shower, how much have you saved? If you save $5 a day when you rent a car from El Cheapo, but it takes 45 minutes to fill out the forms and even longer when you return it, how much of a bargain was it? If you rent, purchase, or lease a car, computer, or appliance, take into account how efficient the service will be when it eventually breaks down.

What about social relationships? Should you hook up with a time-waster? In general, opposites may attract, but they also wear on one another too. Over the long term, opposites tend not to work well if the interaction is intense and constant. A relationship of opposites thrives only if there is strong agreement on some core values.

Exceptions are the highly successful individuals who admit that they aren't very good at time management but their spouse or their secretary or assistant is. Norman Vincent Peale told me that he wasn't good at time management, but his wife and his secretary were. When I asked the chairman of a large corporation if he used a paper organizer or an electronic organizer to help keep him on track, he replied that his organizer was alive. "Her name is Betty," he answered. Other high achievers have made similar statements to me. When I called the office of a nationally famous businessperson to set up an appointment for an interview, I explained that I would be asking for any secrets he might share that saved him time. His appointment secretary replied, "His time-saving secret is me." Obviously, a symbiotic relationship can work quite well.

As a rule, if time is important to you, you will be happiest even in social relationships with people who feel the same way you do about your most valuable asset. These kind of individuals are worth looking for, and they are worth cherishing. Sometimes time-oblivious individuals are absolutely delightful and a joy to be with. Enjoy them as you would any luxury item.

૨૦

LEARN TO DELEGATE

It is better to get 10 people to work than it is to do the work of 10.
—TRADITIONAL SAYING

If somebody else can do it quicker, better, or less expensively than you can, get them to do it. Don't do minimum-wage tasks if you earn more than minimum wage—unless you just enjoy doing them. If raking leaves is fun, do it. Once it becomes a chore, quit. Hire somebody else to do it.

Even if it's not a minimum-wage task, doing it yourself can become a time trap. Repairing your car or doing your own plumbing are examples. If you're good at tinkering or can learn quickly, go ahead and repair the faucet or replace the alternator. But if you're clumsy, don't know what to do, and know that it'll take a long time to learn, pay to get it done. Do such a task only if you have no money at all, or if you get genuine pleasure out of tinkering and feeling good about mastering the challenge.

A recent study has found that American managers and professionals are getting caught in this time trap at work. The research, which involved over 1700 employees in 95 offices, found that managers and professionals are devoting only a small fraction of their work time to the tasks they are hired to do. The director of the study, economist Peter G. Sassone, found that in nearly every office, there were *more* managers and professionals and *fewer* support workers than were required to perform the work cost-effectively.[35]

What does Sassone recommend? Hire support staff to do staff functions. An organization isn't saving money if highly paid professionals are spending lots of time at the photocopying machine and stuffing envelopes.

Whether in the office or at home, consider getting someone to help you.

Delegate to whom?

Staff people and associates

Whenever possible, do *only* what *only* you can do. For example, if you're good at writing proposals, and that's what you're getting paid to do, find someone else to do your photocopying. It's not that you're incapable of doing it, or too proud to do it. It's simply that your assistant can't write the proposal. Do what only you can do. Your assistant can run the photocopier. Your assistant can fetch books from the library. If you are an executive or a manager, you get paid more than assistants. It's an inefficient use of your time to do clerical tasks unless you are the assistant.

Life insurance general agent Sam Rawls says, "I make it a practice to only get involved with clients. Vendors and employees of clients are taken care of by staff. Routine tasks are done by them. Crisis is my responsibility."

Number twos

The director of a large research center recently told me that the success of his program was due as much to having a good number-two person as it was to anything that he himself did. "My assistant does things I'm not good at. For example, he can tell staff people really bad news, and make them feel good about hearing it. I don't know how he does it. And I don't know what I would do without him."

I have heard this kind of comment repeatedly from heads of organizations and units. They are able to thrive as Number One because they have been able to find and keep a good Number Two.

Assistants and managers

Some very successful individuals hire personal assistants. In fact, National Speakers Association president Naomi Rhode considers a personal assistant the most important time-saving asset a busy executive can have. Rhode believes it is crucial to try to find someone who is not just skillful and dependable, but who also has similar values to her own. That way, the assistant can be expected to do an assignment just the way she would do it. Such individuals are not bound by a narrowly written job description. They may make hair appointments, purchase gifts, book flights and hotel accommodations, and schedule limousines.

Judy Thomas, who's been a producer and an assistant for Larry King for over 11 years, has a wide range of responsibilities including booking the talent for his show and being a liaison person between speakers' bureaus and agencies that are interested in scheduling Larry King for events. Thomas has contact with numerous assistants and managers of celebrities. I asked her if there was a common denominator. Thomas replied: "All of us want the best for the person we're working for."

Here are the rules Judy Thomas recommends for people in her position:

- Keep the lines of communication open by setting a time daily to go over the schedule for the day.

- Be dependable and trustworthy. You have to be someone who can pull it all together. The other person has to know that his or her requests are being handled.

- Write all requests down in a journal.

- Reconfirm any engagements. (Thomas personally double-confirms all events the day before they are to occur.)

- Have a sense of humor.

Expediters

An expediter is an expert who can get you through a maze or handle a job for which you don't have the time or knowledge. In New York City, for example, architects and building owners sometimes hire expediters to get permits for construction projects. The rules and regulations are often so complicated and tedious that a specialist is required. The expediters know where to get the necessary forms and how to fill them out. I have hired expediters abroad to help clear shipments through customs. They handle the hassles and I relax.

Interns and co-op students

Consider hiring an intern or a co-op student. Recently a bank president told me that he can't get through all the publications and reading materials that pile up in his office. "If I go away for a few days, there's a stack a foot high." I recommended that he hire an intern to make the initial cut and highlight what seems worth looking at. He and the intern need to invest time at the outset of the assignment so that the intern knows what to look for. But after the project gets under way, the time that he will save through this initial screening can be significant.

Interns and co-op students usually are highly motivated. They're willing to work for modest pay if they can gain useful experience, and they're very teachable. Moreover, it's usually a win-win situation. At the end of the internship, they will be able to list a great reference on their résumés.

Gofers and expediters

A gofer is a low-wage individual who does just what the name implies. They "go for" whatever someone with more power than they needs or wants. Their job description is general and their power is minimal, but their future can be bright because they often interact face-to-face with influential people. If they are talented and resourceful, they may get noticed and promoted. Hiring a gofer can be a successful time tactic in many situations.

Housekeepers and maintenance workers

"Hire a maid," Mary Kay advises her salespeople. It isn't a luxury. It's an economic decision, she explains. You may have to pay $10 to $15 per hour for the maid, but you can make several times that amount selling.

Larry King says that he's a type-A personality who doesn't do well with life's little annoyances: traffic jams, planes that are late, and machines that don't work. Whenever he can, he hires someone to deal with tasks that annoy him. "What I've gotten good at is being willing to pay not to do them," he told me. "I'll hire the handyman to come over to do something I might have been able to do myself."

For him this kind of decision is not based on economics. It's not that Larry King considers his time is higher priced—even though it is—or that he is incapable of doing it himself. "I could be just sitting around for an hour with nothing to do, and I'll still pay to have him do it." The rule is to hire someone else to do it—whenever you can—if doing it is an annoyance. Most careers involve doing some tasks that are boring or unpleasant. Often these tasks come with the job and can't be successfully avoided. But if they can, at work or at home, pay somebody else to do them.

There must be quite a number of people out there who feel just like Larry King does. A whole service industry has grown up around doing tasks that people don't have time for, can't do, or just don't want to do. Employees of these companies will clean your residence, purchase gifts for you, wrap them and mail them, bake birthday cakes and deliver them, care for your lawn, or be your own concierge for an hour or a day. Use them.

Unpaid volunteers

Many organizations, like college alumni associations and religious and philanthropic organizations, use volunteers extensively. Delegating to unpaid volunteers can be much more difficult than delegating to employees because the volunteers don't have to do anything that they don't want to. You have no real authority over them. Getting things done through unpaid volunteers depends upon your power of persuasion and your understanding and use of sociological and psychological principles.

However, astonishing results often come from volunteers. Highly motivated volunteers will sometimes do more than paid employees because of their love for the task or because they feel loyal to the organization or to the person who enlisted them.

How to delegate?

Effective delegation enables you to take on bigger projects than you could alone, spreads the risk, and creates a team spirit.

But delegation can be a two-edged sword. If you don't follow the basic principles of delegation, you may wish that you had done the job yourself. If you delegate to people who are not capable of doing what you ask them to, you will have to retrieve the project and reassign it, or do it yourself. You'll lose time and perhaps make an enemy. In order to increase the likelihood of success, keep these guidelines in mind:

■ *Pick people who can accept responsibility.* Not everyone can. You are in trouble if you think that you can hand off tasks to just anyone, regardless of his or her attitude. Over and over I have heard highly successful people say that they get their work done through others. But almost in the same breath they will add, "Surround yourself with good people." Home Depot CEO Bernie Marcus told me: "If you don't surround yourself with the best people possible, you'll end up having to do everything yourself. So what I've done is to find the people out there who are competent, who are entrepreneurial, the way I am, but per-

haps more organized and people who are not afraid of a challenge, nor are afraid of decision making." That's a big order,
but you can see this theme of looking for certain qualities you
need running through his entire answer.

- *Delegate in terms of the other person's skills and interests.* Try to
  match the person to the task. Appeal to what interests that person. Perhaps the most important sentence in Dale Carnegie's
  How to Win Friends and Influence People is the following: "The
  only way on earth to influence the other fellow is to talk about
  what he wants and show him how to get it."[36]

- *Recognize the reality of the learning curve.* The person performing the task may not do it well at first. You may be tempted to
  take over the project. You will need to weigh the time you
  might lose at first against the time you'll save in the long run.

- *Reduce risks by assigning low-risk projects at first.* This approach
  minimizes the potential damage that can result from failure,
  and it also builds up the confidence level of the person to
  whom you assign a responsibility.

- *Inform the other person why, not simply what.* Otherwise you
  may get automatonlike behavior. When people understand
  how their work fits into the overall process, they're more likely
  to react intelligently if something goes wrong, or if you're not
  around to provide guidance. Also, they're more likely to come
  up with innovations that may make their particular task more
  efficient. Help them see the big picture.

- *Be prepared to let delegatees put their own spin on the assignment.*
  Their way may be an improvement. Be willing to listen to their
  idea, even if you decide not to accept it.

- *Make sure that you communicate.* Be sure that you explain with
  a vocabulary that the other individual can understand. Don't
  use technical jargon unless you are absolutely sure the other
  person knows the terms. Don't talk too quickly. It often helps
  to dictate instructions on a cassette or write them out so that
  the delegatee can recheck the message. There's nothing wrong
  with asking the other person to repeat the instructions. You'll
  sometimes be amazed at what you get back.

- *Keep tabs on what you delegate.* One CEO of a large company put it this way: "Until you have somebody on the same wavelength that you're on, it's very important that you follow up initially because in the translation a lot of things become mixed. You have to be very careful that your message gets through, and the only way to find that out is to check it through all the way." Even if you've received a commitment from someone really competent, and you know you're on the same wavelength, be sure to get progress reports regularly. For example, authors are notorious procrastinators, so a good editor will call periodically just to find out how the project is coming along. The same advice applies to lawyers, who typically have a number of cases pending at any given time and often pay attention to the case that is most urgent. A request for a progress report helps to keep your case from getting buried.

- *Give the task importance.* You're asking for trouble if you say, "This isn't a big deal," or "This is a no-brainer." You'll probably get sloppy work or procrastination, or both. Instead, try saying something like, "I want you to take on a job that's really important for the success of this project." Make it clear that you think the individual selected is precisely the best person to do it. Even if you're asking someone to staple papers for you, emphasize how important for that work to look first-rate.

  It's risky to publicly ask for volunteers for a really important project. The least-qualified person in the room may volunteer. Then what do you do? Remember that good people like to be chosen.

- *Assign priorities and a due date.* When you assign someone else a task, be sure to give a realistic sense of how important it is and when you need it completed. I personally use a numbering system, with number 1 being the most important and number 10 the least important. If I write out an assignment on a note, I pencil in the number at the top of the note.

- *Provide the training necessary for the individual to succeed.* If delegation involves managerial responsibility, and if the person delegated to has little management experience, give that person the time and resources to learn. It takes time to store the necessary patterns in memory. Short courses, self-study programs, cassettes and films, workshops, and mentor programs can help the person make the transition and acquire the necessary database to succeed in the new job. Empowering without training is usually worse than not empowering at all.

- *Limit the span of control.*   The best practitioner of delegation I ever encountered was William H. Souther, who at one time in his career was educational director of a large metropolitan church that attracted thousands of youngsters and adults to its religious classes.

  Souther eventually became a professor and taught classes on the principles of administration, one of which I attended. Souther believed that you could build an organization of thousands on the basis of delegating to units of approximately 8 to 14 people, who would delegate to 8 to 14 people, who in turn delegated to 8 to 14 people. Souther felt that a unit of 8 to 14 people is a manageable size to inform, train, and keep motivated. He didn't like for the accountability units to get much larger than 12 or 14 people. "Using this principle, you can run an organization of a hundred, a thousand, ten thousand," he told us. Souther knew. He had done it.

- *Delegate at appropriate levels.*   Delegation does not have to be an all-or-nothing procedure. Many executives who are known as hands-on managers are effective delegators, too. They delegate total and complete authority for some tasks (i.e., "Proceed, then inform."), yet delegate in steps for other projects (i.e., "Inform, then proceed."). The nature and complexity of the project and the level of development of the delegatee are the key considerations in delegating.

- *Delegate the entire job whenever possible.*   Charles H. Teller, Jr., director of business development for Georgia Gulf Corporation says: "Many people get a kick out of being able to bring back a project neatly tied in a bow. I prefer to delegate the entire job and give people the experience of carrying through. It's frustrating to go nine-tenths of the way and not have any sense of what finally happens to a project. At least give them a chance to make a recommendation about the final outcome."

- *Don't hog the credit.* Start with honest appreciation. "Thank you" is such a simple expression yet it does so much. If you want help from your friends and want to keep on getting help from them, be lavish with your praise. Robert Woodruff, the legendary czar of Coca-Cola for many years, had the following motto displayed in his office for many years: "There is no limit to what a man can do or where he can go if he doesn't mind who gets the credit."

- *Try to help people feel good about themselves.* Bernie Marcus believes this is the best way to keep good people. He believes that an appeal to loyalty to the organization won't work indefinitely. "They have to feel good about what they're doing," Marcus told me. "They have to feel good about their position. They have to feel like they can make mistakes. They have to feel excited every day of their lives." Whenever people don't like themselves, they eventually perform badly.

ॐ

HIRE THE BEST

Pay More and Cry Only Once. (Sign on a plumber's truck in Los Angeles)

Everyone loves a bargain. Occasionally a genuine bargain can be found. A knowledgeable shopper can sometimes purchase a product far below its true value from a seller who's in distress, isn't informed, or doesn't know how to properly market it. Generally, however, you will save time and money if you try to get the best, even if you have to pay a bit more.

The initial cost of employing someone who is truly superb may seem exorbitant at first. But the long-term costs may be less than if you decide to use someone whose rates seem inexpensive. Why? First, you must factor in the time you spend looking for a bargain. Your search time is a cost. Second, if you choose the best person or product, even if the initial cost is higher, you will probably come out far ahead because you will spend less time taking it back if it (or they) don't work, cleaning up the mess, patching it up.

Novices may be earnest and work very hard, but they're actually practicing at your expense. Maybe they'll get it right, maybe they won't. An expert will be able to do more than save you time by knowing what to do and will likely have just the right tool to do it with. You're usually out of luck if you want a Chevy dealer to make a major repair on a Mercedes. The parts won't fit, the specialized tools won't be there. The mechanic won't know what the tolerances are.

If you need a lawyer to protect your rights to a book or song you've written or a concept you've thought of, you can't waste time with a jack-of-all-trades lawyer who spends most of his days doing title searches or writing wills. Such a lawyer might eventually find out what to do, but will be practicing at your expense.

Guy Millner, chairman of the Norrell Corporation, says his best advice to businesspeople is to hire the finest lawyer they can find. "The most expensive lawyer often turns out to be the one that's cheapest," Millner told me. "Many entrepreneurs get with some C player who gives them C advice."

Using the services of anyone other than an expert is not simply costly and time-inefficient, it may be downright dangerous. The part-time mechanic who quoted you a cheap price may get your car out of the garage and back on the freeway, but your brakes may fail. The jack-of-all-trades lawyer you hired cheaply may leave your song or book or idea exposed to the tender mercies of thieves. That nice physician who does major surgery at a county hospital just may leave you paralyzed.

Get the best. Look for quality. Astute buyers in the marketplace don't really care how much time and effort you put into a product. What they care about is the quality of the product. I remember once telling Charlie A. Smithgall, then owner of WCNN, that I spent a great deal of time researching and writing the scripts for my radio feature, "The Achievement Digest." He replied that he didn't doubt that, but he didn't really care how much time it took. "I don't care if it takes you 15 minutes. If it's good, we'll use it. And if it takes you three weeks and it's not good, we won't use it." Smithgall was blunt but correct.

Any time you encounter an attorney, a mechanic, or a professional speaker who consistently charges top dollar and gets it year after year, there's a very good reason. They're worth it.

People who charge more than they or their product are worth will soon be out of business. A free marketplace establishes a price for goods and services, driving down the price of the inferior and the shabby, driving out the incompetent and worthless, driving up the price of the truly excellent.

&

MASTER THE ART OF CONFLICT MANAGEMENT

The subject of human conflict doesn't get much attention in time management books, but it should. Enormous resources are spent in conflict between individuals and between groups. War itself is the most obvious example, where the cost is staggering. But even petty disputes between individuals can be costly. The time, money, and effort spent in the conflict itself, not to mention the mental and emotional cost that's involved mobilizing for conflict and getting over it, can be heavy indeed.

The following are some of the main points to consider if you are serious about reducing the time costs of conflict.

Conflict avoidance.

The least costly way to deal with conflict is to avoid it. Many conflicts are simply not worth having, and with a bit of forethought and prevention, can be stopped before major damage is done. Abraham Lincoln wrote, "Discourage litigation. Persuade your neighbors to compromise whenever you can. Point out to them how the nominal winner is often a real loser in fees, expenses and waste of time."[37]

Take the following steps in order to prevent conflict before it starts:

- Know who you're dealing with. One of the characteristics of Japanese businesspeople is to spend a great deal of time checking out people or firms before embarking on business ventures with them. They intend to do business for a long time and want to make sure mistakes are avoided at the outset. Westerners often find the practice tedious and unnecessarily time-consuming. But it does have its merits. Once a well-investigated relationship is begun, it is more likely to last than one that is hastily arranged.

- Get it in writing. Spell out as many eventual sources of contention as you can anticipate. An old proverb advises: "Good fences make good neighbors."

- Avoid impossible situations. Don't think you are Superman or Wonder Woman. Unless you are an expert at turnaround situations, if really good people have failed, you probably will, too.

- Check out great deals going in. If it sounds too good to be true, it probably is too good to be true. Investigate. Ask for references. Ask hard questions. It's better to risk offending someone than having an economic loss or embarrassment later on.

Solving, resolving, and dissolving conflicts.

Sometimes it's impossible to avoid a conflict. "Beware of entrance to a quarrel," Shakespeare wrote, "but being in, bear it, that the opposed may beware of thee." If you do find yourself in a quarrel, here are some guidelines that you may want to follow.

- Reexamine the issue and make sure you know just what the conflict really is about.

- Do you really want to fight now or is there a better time to try to resolve this confict?

- Listen to the other party and respect his point of view.

- Try to remain calm and reasonable no matter how angry the other party may be.

- Restate the other party's position.

This last tactic is sometimes called a "crossover" discussion. In a crossover discussion, each participant listens without interrupting while the other expresses his or her views. Continue to do this until each person can state the other's position in a way that is acceptable to each party. The benefit of this exercise is that it diverts energy from raw argument into fact gathering.

Exit from the conflict circle.

According to research data gathered by the Marriage and Families Studies Group at Catholic University in Washington, D.C., happy couples often disagree as frequently as unhappy ones. The difference is that the happy couples are far better at ending spats—"exiting," the researchers call it.

In both instances, there will be exchanges of negative behaviors at the beginning of the encounter—criticism for criticism, harsh word for harsh word. The "happy" couples will go round and round for two or three "loops" or exchanges. Then one partner will become more positive and begin to move out of the loop. "Unhappy" couples will go round and round the loop, sometimes for as many as a dozen times, and each time they do, they elaborate the negative theme. They wear a dark, frayed circle into the emotional and mental fabric of the relationship.[38]

Use a third party.

Gene Dunwody owns a successful architecture firm in Macon, Georgia. When I interviewed him about what he is really good at, he replied, "Listening." He explained, "I don't have a lot of creative flair. My son, who works here, does. Several of my people do. What I'm really good at is listening. You see, sometimes the client and the builder will get into a dispute over something. Because I can hear what they both are saying, I can often find common ground."

That's the great advantage a third party has. They sometimes can find common ground. The use of third parties can be as informal as talking to a friend or a marriage counselor or as formal as going into arbitration, where rules and procedures are very specific.

If you use a third party, several criteria are essential: (1) The third party must be credible to both sides. That involves being impartial. (2) The third party should be skillful. A clumsy third party can make matters worse. In addition to facilitating skills, it helps if they have some background in the area of dispute. (3) They will need a large dose of an intangible quality called *judgment*.

You may need to use an attorney. There are many situations in which a good attorney is absolutely essential. Sometimes a letter drafted by a respected attorney or a phone call will bring the conflict to a halt. If you have a lawyer with a formidable reputation, that reputation will often scare off opponents and make them willing to settle. Attorneys are often at their best doing behind-the-scenes work, finding the basis for compromise. If a courtroom looms, be sure to have a professional at your side except for the smallest problems. Don't waste time trying to negotiate through unfamiliar territory. There's an old saying to the effect that he who represents himself in court has a fool for a client.

Arbitrate.

Too many people think of suing and going to court as a first option to settling conflict. Litigation should be the last option. Arbitration is a time-effective alternative to litigation. Litigation is rarely prompt. Six months to a year is considered rapid in many courts. There are inherent delays. You may be number 12 on the calendar, but you must bring all your witnesses and be ready just in case the other cases are settled quickly. There are numerous false starts.

In order to deal with this problem, several arbitration and mediation organizations have been created during the past few years. Some are nationwide. These organizations provide benefits that a public court can't. Former Judge R. Keegan Federal, Jr., describes these benefits: "You get your case scheduled at a time and date which is convenient for you and all the other parties. There are no delays because yours is the only case scheduled for that time. There are no false starts because everyone involved agrees in advance on the hearing date. And you don't have to pay your lawyer and your witnesses for getting ready over and over again."

Say good-bye to water under the bridge.

One of the biggest costs of conflict is the time many people spend worrying about the conflict after it has occurred. You must learn to let some things go. There are some battles that you will not win. Fred P. Burke, an Atlanta entrepreneur, says, "If you keep looking back and second-guessing, and wondering 'If we had done this instead of that,' then you'll never ever succeed. You must take advantage of the water under the bridge to make better decisions in the future but you cannot get back the water. It's gone and you are going to have to be happy with that, or, if not happy, at least recognize that it's gone forever more."

There are some blunders that you will not be able to remedy. You can waste as much time worrying about things that are irretrievable as you lose in the actual conflicts themselves. Regret is an enfeebling emotion.

❧ 12 ❧

Invest Time to Save Time

❧

SHARPEN THE AXE

If I had eight hours to chop down a tree, I'd spend six hours sharpening an axe. —TRADITIONAL SAYING

The first day the young lumberman cut down 10 trees. His axe was keen and he was strong and fresh. The second day, he worked just as hard. In fact, he felt that he worked even harder than the first day. But only eight trees fell.

Tomorrow, he would get an earlier start. So he retired early and the next morning worked as hard as he could, but managed to cut down only seven trees.

The following day, he was down to five trees. The fifth day, he managed to chop down only three trees, and was exhausted by nightfall. Early the next morning, he was chopping away furiously when an old man passed by and asked, "Why don't you stop and sharpen your axe?"

"I can't. I'm too busy chopping down trees," he replied.

Most of us have behaved like the lumberman at some point in our lives. We got so caught up in an activity that we didn't take the steps necessary to make the work easier and quicker.

I continued to use a typewriter for years after word processors were available. I listened to writers and editors praise computers.

They said that they didn't know what they would do without them. "One day I'll learn," I promised myself, while continuing to churn out letters and articles the proven way thousands of great writers had done it before me.

Then one day I decided to take the plunge. The word processing software I chose, unfortunately, was not user-friendly. It was user-vicious. So learning proved to be a painful, often traumatic experience. During that period letters and other needed tasks went undone. But I could quickly catch up after mastering the new skill.

At times, I was tempted to go back to the typewriter. But I persevered, and now I am one of those people who delight in what this wonderful tool called the computer can do.

Today, learning to use a computer is not difficult at all. Better software, training videos, picture icons, and user-friendly equipment have made using the computer fun. But when I learned, sharpening the axe was not pleasant at all.

The initial cost of axe sharpening is not just time, it's money, too. The sharpening process may mean purchasing books, tapes, and equipment, and taking courses. Sharpening the axe may mean relocating to a place where you can perfect your craft, hone your skill with the best teachers, with state-of-the-art equipment.

Avail yourself of opportunities to upgrade your skills and learn new ones. Your employer may even help out. Many companies reimburse employees for the cost of taking advanced courses, especially if they have some relation to the job. If no one will reimburse you, do it anyway. Here are some ways you can invest in yourself:

- Join trade and professional associations. Attend their conferences and workshops.
- Read publications in your field that you don't have to read.
- Take a speed-reading course.
- Enroll in an executive training program at a well-regarded business school.
- Learn how to make your computer do more than the basics.
- Learn another language.

- Take a night course in a subject that has always interested you but you never had time to pursue.

- Take time to do small tasks that will make you more efficient, like spending a few moments to program your phone to automatically dial a number that you call frequently.

You will find that chopping with a sharp axe is more fun and less time-consuming than working yourself to death with a dull one. The next tactic is recommended only for readers who understand the principle of the sharp axe.

❧

BECOME AN EXPERT

Capability precedes competence, which precedes proficiency, and finally comes mastery. —SUBHASH KAMAT

Somebody once asked the great writer Flannery O'Connor, "Why do you write?" She replied, "Because I'm good at it." O'Connor wasn't being arrogant. She was simply telling the inquirer what a teacher had told her years earlier—that she could be a very good writer. She had worked hard and had become an expert at her craft.

You save time by becoming an expert. The expert doesn't start from scratch when a new client comes in the door. The expert already has a database of knowledge from which to begin.

When people first start out in a field, they have to acquire a vocabulary. Gradually, as they work at it, they build up their vocabulary. They don't have to grope for words. One day, they realize they are articulate in their field. They're confident of their ability in their specialized area. They're like Charles Schulz, who told me he didn't know how good he was at drawing, but said he, "I'm really an expert in the comic strip as a medium."

If you're not yet at this level of proficiency—if you can't honestly say that you're an expert at anything—you may want to learn about a word that my friend Jim Wesley believes in. Wesley, former president and CEO of the Summit Communications Group, told me that several years ago he was having dinner with a prominent physician, and asked this question: "Why is it that some physicians become truly excellent and others never quite make it?" The physician replied: "If you want to be an excellent physician, you must *embrace* your field."

Wesley told me he has never forgotten the word the physician used: *embrace.* "You must embrace your field." Wesley says that's been true in his own career. When he started managing radio business for Cox Communications, Wesley remembers wanting to learn everything about radio from the ground up. As he put it, "I wanted to know the feel of the goods. Whatever brainpower I acquired in college, those were just disciplines that supported my knowledge of the field."

Wesley also told me how he does the research that helps him embrace the field. "I ask for everything and throw out what I don't want." Some people ask for too little at the beginning or their request is too selective. Wesley says, "In the beginning, you really don't know what to ask for. So ask for everything."

This kind of study sounds like a lot of work, a lot of time invested. It is. But think of the time spent in a field as an *investment.* If your initial investment is tiny, you should not expect large dividends. But if you choose your investment carefully, and then make a major commitment of time to it, you can draw handsome dividends the rest of your life.

Even if you change fields, you may be able to use chunks of information and skill that you acquired in your former field of expertise. You certainly will be able to use the learning skills that you acquired. And the confidence you gained mastering one area will serve you well in your new undertaking.

The benefits of becoming an expert, in terms of time tactics, are substantial:

- Experts don't begin from a standing start. They already have a database from which to draw. They usually know other experts in the field who can help them if they need assistance.

- Experts are more likely than the average person to go to the heart of a problem, more likely to be able to distinguish between frills and substance, between symptoms and cause. That's always a time-saver.

- Experts know their limitations. This knowledge will enhance your success-failure ratio. Famed guitarist Chet Atkins told me that in order to be successful, you must recognize your strong points and your weak points and work within those limitations.

- Experts have the right tools. There's an old saying, "The mark of an expert is his tools." An expert will have the right wrench, software package, or reference book to do the job.

If you sell securities, become an expert on municipal bonds, or mutual funds, or some other specialty. If you sell real estate, spend an extra hour a day learning everything there is to know about a certain area of the city, or become an expert on condominiums or warehouses.

Discover the fundamental truth that Flannery O'Connor learned. Do what you're good at until you are an expert at it. Efficiency is one of many benefits that come with mastery.

❧
ONE EXTRA HOUR A DAY CAN WORK LIKE MAGIC

Employ your time improving yourself by other men's writings so that you shall come easily by what others have labored hard for. —SOCRATES

In 1972, Jim Cathcart was a struggling salesman. That year he happened to hear a radio program produced by Earl Nightingale. Nightingale made a statement that revolutionized the young salesman's life: "If you'll spend one extra hour each day in the study of your chosen field...you'll be a national expert in five years or less."

Cathcart took the saying to heart. "Within five years, just as Nightingale had told me, I was traveling the nation speaking, training, and writing on my chosen subject," Cathcart stated recently. Today Cathcart is one of the nation's best-known personalities in the field of personal development and a past president of the National Speakers Association.

Auto-leasing expert Dick Biggs told me that he never heard Earl Nightingale, but for years he made himself read all the trade journals in his field for at least an hour a day. That reading was in addition to doing the actual work that was required in the business. Biggs started his own leasing business in 1982 and a little less than five years later began to be called upon to tell what he had learned to manufacturers, dealerships, and financial institutions.

Nightingale's promise calls for an *extra* hour per day, not simply an hour per day. The promise begins when you invest an hour beyond what it takes to be simply adequate.

The extra hour makes the difference. Why? Because it's so rare to find anyone who puts in much extra effort at anything for an extended period of time. If you discount the brief spurts of energy following New Year's resolutions and the like, most people, most of the time, do just enough to keep from being embarrassed.

I've spent a lot of time interviewing the top people of the world, and truthfully, most of them are not that much more impressive than many of their peers. They're just a little bit better, but they've been just a little bit better year after year for quite a while. That gives them more than a little edge on the competition.

The extra-hour principle will work for you whenever you begin to use it, even at the very beginning of a career. A young person I know went for a job interview armed with information from a database. She was responding to an advertisement for a sales position at one of the big photocopying companies.

Prior to the interview, she had gone to the library to find the annual report of the company. There, she found much more than an annual report. A database provided her with inside information about the company. She was able to go into the interview with a thorough knowledge of the company.

During the interview, she mentioned two or three items she had learned and eventually showed the interviewer the computer printout. The person interviewing her for the job, a regional sales manager, was astonished at what she knew. He also was impressed by the interest that she showed in the company. The printout contained information that even he didn't know—and he had been with the company for 15 years. He spent the next day holed up in his office studying the report. And the applicant got the job.

Computer software executive Leland Strange does research as a survival technique. "I have lots of people working for me, but I guarantee you that not one of them spends more time in a month reading the technical journals than I do." In high-technology fields, today's leader can be breathing somebody else's dust a scant six months from now.

Zig Ziglar told me that he has spent an average of three hours a day reading for the past 25 years. As one of the best-known motivational speakers and authors in the nation, Ziglar could be tempted to coast on his past reputation. But instead, he will spend several hours polishing and incorporating new material into a presentation that he has made many times previously.

Some people don't think of research as a time tactic because they are in a hurry to do something. Reading a "reference book" somehow doesn't seem like *doing* anything. But doing research is work, perhaps the most important work you will do. We even have a word for it that implies that it is work. We say, "Do your home*work*."

The "extra hour" formula works especially well if the hour is one of focused study. An expert, by definition, is someone who knows more about a given topic than most other people. If you learn more than most people about a subject—any subject—you have an edge.

It takes discipline to study the extra hour, day after day, week after week. In fact, the discipline itself may contribute as much to your ultimate success as the knowledge gained.

There is a sense in which there is no way to *save* time. You can't hoard it or put it back for a later day. You have to use it as it comes, but you can invest it for later use.

At hydroelectric plants, the demand for power doesn't remain constant. It's highest on hot days of summer when air conditioners are running full blast. It's usually low during the middle of the night. Yet the capacity of the plant to generate power remains more or less constant.

What to do with the excess electricity? The technology for storing it in batteries is limited. One solution some engineers have come up with is to use excess electricity during nonpeak hours to pump water that has flowed through the turbines back up into the lake behind the dam. A lake full of water is power held in reserve.

Knowledge is like that lake of water behind the dam—power waiting to be released. People who invest time every day becoming proficient are storing up power for future use.

Don't leave the extra hour a day to chance. Get it on your calendar. Make an appointment with yourself to do it.

GET IT RIGHT

Measure twice so you have to cut only once. —TRADITIONAL SAYING

U.S. Supreme Court Justice Sandra Day O'Connor often has to make decisions that are bound to upset lots of people, regardless of the position she takes. It's a part of her everyday life to confront thorny issues like abortion, gun control, civil rights, and capital punishment—issues that evoke impassioned feelings.

How does she sleep at night, knowing that some of what she does will be so controversial? She answered my question this way:

> We have many items on our plates at all times as judges. I can work on only one at a time, and when I work on one, *I give it my full attention* and I do the best I can with it. Then I go on to something else. One thing that I've learned as a judge—certainly as a trial judge when I first went on the bench and I've never changed—and that is to just do the best I can and not look back. Not look back to see, "Oh, did I make the right decision?" "Was that right?" I do not do that. I put all the time and effort at the front end in trying to decide it correctly in the first place and do the best I can. Then I don't look back and have regrets or agonize over it. I may have to live with the consequences, but I'm

going to live with them without regrets, because I did the best I could with it at the time.

Sandra Day O'Connor has learned to do it right the first time because she may not have the opportunity to do it over again.

Likely as not you won't do everything right the first time. But you can follow procedures to make sure it's right before you let it go. Actually, what's important is not so much doing it right as getting it right.

The word *right* doesn't mean perfect. Austin McGonigle says: "Most of us grew up hearing the phrase, 'If you're going to do something, do it right.' Regrettably, I find many people interpret the word *right* to mean *perfect*. Misinterpreting this saying can cause people not to start projects until they are ready to do it perfectly. They procrastinate instead of getting started." If you wait for perfection, you will never start and you may never let it go. Getting it right means reducing the number of errors to acceptable parameters.

Here are some fundamental tactics to do that:

- *Triple-check the results.* Checking it thrice may run against your temperament. You may be so tired of what you've just produced that you want to get onto something else. But go over it again.

  The late Dr. Vernon Crawford, a physicist and former chancellor of the university system of Georgia, made it a practice to read his manuscripts and reports backward. Reading backward is slow going and requires discipline, but Crawford said it's highly effective.

- *Check spellings.* Ruby Wagner, one of my English literature teachers in college, enforced a rule, which at the time I felt was harsh. Any paper that had three misspelled words received an automatic *F*, regardless of how well it was written. I never completely agreed with her approach and still don't. Nevertheless, here's how Wagner defended her rule: "All of you can't be great writers," she would say, "but each one of you has the ability to look up words in a dictionary. So don't turn in a paper with misspellings—even if you have to look up every word."

Today most software packages have excellent spellcheck and stylecheck programs. These programs are not 100 percent accurate because usage varies and the English language is so unpredictable. A spellcheck program won't tell you whether to use "compliment" or "complement," "whether" or "weather." Some stylecheck programs will catch some of these errors, but don't rely on them completely.

The following poem, which circulated through Coastal Corporation in Houston, demonstrates that software can make sure words are spelled correctly, but can't insure (or ensure) that they are used correctly.

I have a spelling checker.

It came with my PC.

It plainly marks four my revue,

Mistakes I cannot sea.

I've run this poem threw it,

I'm sure you're please to no.

It's letter perfect in it's weigh,

My checker tolled me sew.

Consider spellcheck and stylecheck as a valuable *first cut* in getting it right.

Don't assume anything about the spelling of proper names. Names can be notorious villains. Reference books are useful but not 100 percent accurate either. Sometimes you'll need to contact an expert.

- *Check definitions.* You don't want to be a Mrs. Malaprop, the woman in Sheridan's *The Rivals* who constantly made ridiculous blunders with the words she used (for example, making reference to an "alligory" in the Nile River).

- *If you are called upon to make a presentation and must use an expression or a name, call an expert before going public.* If it's the name of a movie or an actor, call the film critic at a major newspaper. If it's a composer, call the music department of a university or someone who's knowledgeable at a big record store.

- *Check style and usage.* If you do any writing at all, acquire two invaluable aids: *The New York Times Manual of Style and Usage,* revised and edited by Lewis Jordan, and *The Associated Press Style Book and Libel Manual.* Any good bookstore will be able to obtain both of them for you.

  These are the reference books that editors and writers have on their shelves. They indicate when to use a hyphen, when to capitalize, and when to abbreviate, plus they answer hundreds of other questions that come up in the nature of writing reports and articles and business letters. They are chock full of information.

  I once undertook reading *The New York Times Manual of Style and Usage* from cover to cover. It sounds like a boring thing to do, but it turned out to be enjoyable and informative reading.

- *Form a partnership with someone who's methodical and careful.* If you are one who tends not to pay attention to small print and minor details, find people to help you who do. Pay them. That way you have a better claim on their services. If you depend on volunteers to proof your work, what can you say if they let something serious slip by?

  Even when you have more than one person proofing, errors will still slip by. One way to cut down on errors is to have one proofreader start from the back of a document and the other from the front. People tend to get tired as they read, so this ensures that the end of the manuscript will be read as carefully as the beginning.

  Editors, proofreaders, and verifiers have saved me more than once. A verifier at *The New York Times* caught a mistake in a story a famous football coach told me about a game his team had played in. The coach should have known the details about an incident that occurred in one of his games, but his memory was faulty. The verifier saved everyone from embarrassment.

  I know a director of marketing at a large TV network who hires a freelance editor to go over all important copy before it goes into print. She told me that the people in her unit are very strong creatively, but not particularly strong writers. "If we make a mistake and we have to reprint a brochure, it might cost $20,000. We'll spend $100 to have someone look over everything so that doesn't happen."

Some individuals are in such a hurry to get on with things that they do sloppy work. They confuse quantity with quality. A university administrator I know, who's very bright, is nonetheless impulsive and not thorough in his analysis. His colleagues say (behind his back) that he lives by the motto: "Ready, fire, aim." That approach can be costly, time consuming, and dangerous to whatever the gun is pointed at.

WRITE IT DOWN

A short pencil is better than a long memory. —TRADITIONAL SAYING

Your mind can be conditioned to work for you all the time if it knows that you're going to make use of its efforts. At the very least, carry paper and pen with you, perhaps some 3 × 5 index cards. Portable computers are becoming more portable all the time and are increasingly useful as data savers, retrievers, and transmitters.

Musician, comedian, and media personality Steve Allen takes a tape recorder with him everywhere he goes. If an idea for a book or an article occurs to him, he will dictate it on the spot. If the tune for a new song comes to him, he will find a piano and record it.

Don't write down everything. If you do, you'll have such a mass of notes that you probably will never go back to them and use them. Professional speaker and trainer Terry Paulson recommends "keeper pages." If you attend a conference, limit yourself to one page on which you write all the things that you plan to do or use. Paulson retains these keeper pages for later review. If he is on hold on the phone, he will pull out one of the keeper pages and read it. Because Paulson deliberately limits himself to writing only the ideas that he can use, the page is worth reading again. "If you don't review your notes at all, you lose about 70 percent in three or four days," Paulson says. "If you review at least once, you reverse the ratio."

Ideas often come to creative people at unexpected times and unexpected places. Jonas Salk, the creator of the Salk vaccine for polio and the founder of the Salk Clinic, kept journals of the ideas that came to him in the night. This way, he accumulated hundreds of pages of notes that gave him ideas about science, society, and philosophy.

Be prepared. I've seen people go into appointments, often with people who were very important to their careers, without a pen and pad.

Just think what one good idea per meeting or convention over a lifetime would be worth if you had retained them. People pay good money to attend conferences and seminars and go to sessions without a pen and pad. Perhaps they expect nothing worthwhile will be communicated. Perhaps they plan to memorize everything that is important.

Learn to write down the details of mundane transactions. Not long ago, a professional speaker was in Colorado to make a presentation to a large conference at one of the beautiful lodges in the ski country. His room was provided on a complimentary basis by the hotel for two nights, because he was the keynote speaker.

When he checked in, he noticed that one night instead of two nights had been typed on his form. He asked if the desk clerk would look into the matter. Not long after he reached his room, the phone rang. The assistant manager was on the other end: "Yes, you were right. Your room is comped for two nights." She said that she would make the change. No problem.

Two days later, when he checked out, he looked at his bill and noticed that he was comped for one day, not two. He told the clerk at the counter, "Your assistant manager assured me that you were not charging for the second day." She replied, "Which assistant manager? We have five." He told her that it was a young woman. She replied, "We have three women who are assistant managers." They had to begin anew, track down someone who knew about the commitment, and change the bill.

Eventually the matter was settled, but after many minutes had been wasted.

What was his mistake? He had not taken the time to write down the assistant manager's name. This kind of omission almost always costs time. And it did in his case. He had to find a new person and begin the negotiation all over again from scratch.

When you talk business, if somebody quotes a price or a rate or makes an agreement, ask for that person's name. Then write it down and the specifics. That way, when you call back, you don't have to start all over again.

Make notes on every transaction that could have significance later on. I have created a simple system in my computer with a file that I call "Journal." Whenever I have a conversation with someone or learn anything that could be useful in the future, I enter it in the file. The results have been wonderful. I make no attempt to organize the material. It's much like a stream of consciousness. But with my computer's search function I can retrieve names and dates and specific details. It puts me in the catbird seat to say, "On April 12, you said you would ship thus and so at such and such a price."

This basic idea comes from two people: Mark McCormack and David Rockefeller. I learned from McCormack to write down information on paper—to keep a journal. I did that for a year or so in notebooks. But I eventually found that it's much more efficient to do it on the computer, because with a computer I can use the search function.

For example, if I'm going to have a meeting with Ron Allen, the CEO of Delta Air Lines, I go to my computer and search for every contact I've had with him—under the name of Allen or Delta. Within a few moments, I know everything that's been transacted between us in the past several years.

From David Rockefeller I learned how valuable a lifetime filing system can be. Rockefeller kept files of index cards on all the people he met, arranged by name and place of residence. He updated the names continually. At the time of my interview, his collection came to many thousands of names. He was going to Boston the day following our interview. His secretary had pulled the cards of all the people who were likely to be at that meeting. "I'll be able to go up to people and ask them about their wife and children or details about their work....people are always pleased if you remember having seen them. My memory isn't that good. It needs a few props."

A computerized journal is a terrific prop. You write it down and you can retrieve the information almost instantly.

⁊⊛

LEARN THE RULES OF THE GAME

If you expect to win in any organization, you must learn what its rules are. Some of these rules may be written, some unwritten. Some of the rules will be mandatory, others optional.

If you break some rules, hardly anyone will notice. But if you violate deeply held taboos, you can end your career and be thrown out of the organization. Understanding the rules can help you function efficiently in an organization. Failure to do so can result in innumerable roadblocks, frustrations, and wasted effort and time. Here are some suggestions about rule-keeping:

- *Read whatever you can that's relevant.* If anything has been written about the specific situation, start by reading that. Even generic material can be helpful. For starters, consider reading *Robert's Rules of Order.* If you haven't read and mastered the basic principles in this important book—and if you participate in a leadership capacity in an organization—it's a must read. If you know the principles well, it will give you an advantage in most organizations.

  Of course, Robert's rules are general, not specific. Many organizations have their own procedures. In actual practice, a group may deviate widely from its own rules. But it's important to know what standard form is.

  If you're a manager, acquaint yourself with the big, fat book of job descriptions, sample forms, and standard operating procedures (SOP) to be found in most large organizations. Knowing or not knowing them can mean the difference between getting things done and having them come back to do over again. In many organizations, if you don't fill out every line, or use the right form, your efforts may be rejected like a worn-out dollar bill in a coin-changing machine.

Find out what is absolutely required. If you are applying for a mortgage, and don't produce all the required papers to the loan administrator, you'll have to go back and find them. Period. More and more companies rely on the computer, which will reject your material if even one item is left out.

- *Keep your eyes and ears open.* Watch who gets punished and rewarded, who gets chosen for office and honors, who gets shunned. Listen carefully and you'll often be able to pick up on the attitudes, concerns, and dominant values of the members. Norms and values are living, dynamic forces in organizations, not just rules written down in books.

- *Find a mentor.* If you can cultivate a friendship with an old hand in a group, do it. People with experience may be willing to share their knowledge with you, help you make the right moves, keep you from blundering, and help you gain forgiveness if you do.

- *Rely on your previous experience.* A Rotary Club in Florida will be similar to one in Kansas. A university in Maine will be similar to one in California, a country club in Virginia to one in Arizona. The names of the players will be different, but the patterns will be similar.

But remember that your previous experience in a similar organization is no automatic guarantee of success. Even if there are similarities, the differences can be dramatic. In Congress, for example, the rules in the U.S. House of Representatives are different from those in the U.S. Senate. "I thought what I had learned in eight years of service in the House might give me a leg up," Vice President Albert Gore, Jr., once commented, "but I found instead that I had to unlearn a lot of the procedures that had seemed to be the same. There are more invisible walls you can bump your nose into in the Senate...unwritten rules that take time to learn."

ご

DON'T WAIT UNTIL IT BREAKS
TO FIX IT

A stitch in time saves nine. —ENGLISH PROVERB

Do it before you really need to. One morning not long ago, I dropped off my car for service. Later the service manager called. The mechanic had noticed that the belts on my engine were beginning to show wear. Did I want them replaced?

My first reaction was to revert to the style of my earlier impoverished years when I would let belts fray until they held on by only a few strands. I also know that unscrupulous mechanics can make a lot of money replacing parts that don't need replacing. So I hesitated.

Then I remembered a Sunday afternoon years ago when a fan belt had snapped on an isolated stretch of highway, far from any town or city. Hours passed before service arrived. Remembering that experience, I told the service manager to go ahead and replace the belts. A painful experience, when recalled, can be a great teacher.

Do it before you absolutely need to. If you replace cartridges, and batteries, and special bulbs before you need them, you'll save time and dollars trying to find them when they burn out. Don't burn up $2.00 worth of gas and $10.00 worth of time driving to find an ink cartridge for $1.29, only to find that they sold out of ink cartridges yesterday.

Do it before you need to is another way of saying, avoid management by crisis. Good time tacticians try to anticipate crises and take steps to prevent them.

If you do preventive maintenance, you'll not get all the wear you might get if you stretch everything to the blowout, breakdown, wearout stage. But the alternative isn't very much fun.

ટૈ**ਛ**

DON'T THINK IT HAS TO BE BROKEN TO IMPROVE IT

The quality movement that's had such an impact on American industry got its start when statistician W. Edwards Deming couldn't find much of an audience for his ideas in the United States following World War II. Deming finally found a job in Japan, where he taught Japanese industrialists to apply statistical quality controls to their manufacturing systems.

One of the lessons Deming emphasized was to constantly improve the system. Taking Deming's words to heart, the Japanese manufacturers achieved standards of excellence previously thought to be unattainable. Those achievements shook American companies out of a complacent, leave-well-enough-alone attitude.

Even American companies that had excellent reputations were challenged. "We thought we were already a good company, and we were," Thomas J. Malone, president of Milliken & Co., told me. "But what we saw the Japanese doing with less-sophisticated equipment knocked our socks off."

Milliken immediately embarked upon an excellence program that included a major thrust aimed at continuous improvement. In 1989 Milliken & Co. won the prestigious Malcolm Baldrige National Quality Award.

Doing hard thinking about ways to improve systems, equipment, and relationships that are performing well can often be an effective time tactic. Eliminating out-of-control episodes is not just money and material resources saved, it's time saved.

❧ 13 ❧

Plan Ahead

❧

THINK THROUGH, THEN FOLLOW THROUGH

If you use your head, you won't have to use your feet as much.

When I was a small boy, my father and I liked to play checkers. But he always managed to win, except when he deliberately played sloppily. My problem was that I was thinking only of the next move, and would stumble into the traps that he had set for me. He would willingly give up one piece knowing that he would take two or three of my pieces a move or two later. He won because he was able to think several moves ahead. After thinking through, my father followed through.

That's what successful people in every field try to do. They anticipate what will work and what will not work and how much time, effort, and resources it will take. If you mentally walk through each step in the project, perhaps using pencil and paper to assist you, you will be able to anticipate what resources you will need and when you will need them. If you don't, you may find yourself midway into the project without some resource you need to complete it. That can mean costly delays or even complete failure.

This is such a basic idea, yet it's ignored every day. We've all seen hopelessly designed buildings and equipment. We ask ourselves how could such things happen? They happen because the people who create them don't do a mental walk-though.

Thinking through and following through is a fundamental principle that can apply to many activities. A workshop participant told me that *before* each staff meeting, he sends an outline of the meeting to all attendees. That outline includes the purpose of the meeting, background material (when appropriate), plus questions, problems, and goals. He has found that getting this outline out prior to the meeting saves time at the meeting because the attendees get into problem solving faster.

Jazz musician Ramsey Lewis told me that he makes it a practice to sit quietly by himself just before he goes on stage and go through the entire concert in his mind. Lewis visualizes what will happen with each number that he will play—just how he will do it, how long it will take, and how the audience will react to it. "After I do that," he told me, "I can't wait to go out and get started."

Think about what you might *need* to do a task. An obvious example: If you itemize your income tax deductions, you will eventually need to sort your receipts. Time tacticians do their sorting all year long. They create separate folders for all the essential categories *beforehand* and file their receipts as they come in. Then, at tax time, it's a simple matter to bring them all together.

Some high achievers allot a specific chunk of time on their to-do list to think through what they are contemplating doing. This gives them time to think about whether they want to move in one direction or the other, and whether they are stumbling into a trap.

Thinking through need not be a solitary task. In fact, for some activities, it is highly recommended to have a coworker. One of the contributions such a colleague can make is to help the partner anticipate what might be needed, what might go wrong, what might happen if x is done instead of y.

Sort the details.

Mary Poole deals with details by sorting them. Thousands of memos, letters, and solicitations find their way to her desk. When I asked how she managed, she replied, "I sort."

Poole tries to handle each piece of paper only once. If she picks up a piece of paper, like a letter or a memo, or a report, she does something with it. She doesn't just put it back down.

Poole sorts paper into three piles. One pile contains items that need to be dealt with immediately. The second pile contains items that are not as urgent but still are important. The third pile contains items that can be read at her leisure. So she actually ends up handling some pieces of paper twice—once to see which pile it goes in and the second time to actually deal with it. But she doesn't do that continual shuffling that so many people engage in.

Sorting paper into three piles seems like such an insignificant tactic. Doing something with a letter once you pick it up seems insignificant, too. But the concept is based on deep and fundamental principles.

Kay Koplovitz sorts into a half-dozen brightly colored folders. Here's the way the system works for Koplovitz. "I have my information that comes into me divided into different colored folders so that the same color is used for internal memos, external mail....Organizations each have their own color folder, and we all know what order of priority those are. So, if I'm pressed for time, I can go right to the important information—the 'must see today' information."

The sorting procedure that Poole and Koplovitz use shows that they both have a system of priorities in place. As we have seen again and again, having priorities and working those priorities is so important. Every letter, magazine, or memo that's stuffed in your mailbox or placed on your desk doesn't have the same importance. If you treat them all alike, you will work very hard, but trivia will get the same attention as material that is vital. A three-pile sort also says there's some structure to what you do. Your work is not random, haphazard, or simply left to chance. Doing something with paper on your desk once you pick it up is a good rule to follow because it saves the little driblets of time. It's thrifty.

Most of us are careful about the big time-wasters—the huge chunks of time that can get away from us if we are not careful. But life can get away from us through thousands of little dribs and dabs, too. Looking at a letter and putting it back down without doing anything about it may consume only a few seconds, a minute or so at best. That's not much time. But if you do that 10 times a day, you will have spent a lot of time shuffling paper in the course of a year.

An undetected leaky faucet can run your water bill up as much as a ruptured pipe would. Why? Because you will take emergency measures to repair the broken pipe, but the leaky faucet wastes the resource drop by drop, hour by hour, month by month, year by year.

Orchestrate the details.

A major symphony orchestra effectively coordinates many individual performers, sometimes well over a hundred. These individual artists and the various sections of strings, woodwinds, brass, and percussion all have separate responsibilities. They may rehearse as individuals or as sections. But when performance time comes, the individuals and the sections can respond as one because all the players have their own copy of the score, which tells them what everyone else is doing. The score—the plan—doesn't stifle virtuosity. It simply raises it to a higher level. The key to the successful orchestration of anything—from producing a movie, coaching a championship football team, or conducting a symphony—involves creating a score, and letting the people involved know the score.

Stanley Kubrick, the filmmaker who produced *Doctor Strangelove, 2001, A Space Odyssey, The Shining,* and *A Clockwork Orange,* orchestrates every aspect of the films that he makes— from the travel plans to the details of each day's shooting. He's like Alfred Hitchcock in that respect. Hitchcock blocked out the smallest and most intricate detail in every scene.

The way directors make this approach work is to see the entire movie in their heads before they begin shooting. What was seen in their heads is meticulously transferred to paper. Deviation is permitted only for an emergency. Making sure everyone is ready to move on cue requires precise planning and management.

Granted, every filmmaker is not as attentive to the small details as Stanley Kubrick or Hitchcock. Some very good producers and directors allow a great deal of latitude, and some of them improvise effectively on the set. But Kubrick, and Hitchcock before him, demonstrate that careful orchestration can move the concept from idea to film with minimum loss.

Bobby Ross, head coach of the Detroit Lions, follows the same approach that Kubrick does. In fact, observers have often commented that practice under Bobby Ross looks like a theatrical production. When Ross was a college coach, one of my students who worked as his assistant described what a practice session was like. Ross produced a schedule each day that included precise assignments for the location of every position and their respective coaches—down to the minute. Practice began and ended at exactly the time listed on the practice schedule. Whenever scrimmage was planned, everyone on the field knew exactly what plays were going to be run and in what order. When he sounded the horn, everybody immediately moved to a designated place on the practice field.

John Wooden, the greatest college basketball coach of all time, elevated orchestration to an art form. Wooden waited 15 years before he won his first NCAA championship, but he won 10 during his last 12 years at UCLA. That feat has never been equaled in basketball history.

Listen to the way Kareem Abdul-Jabbar described practices under Wooden: "Every drill had a precise purpose and was precisely timed. You would advance from one drill to the next and to the next, without stopping or doubling back to repeat a drill. Every workout was a tightly structured grid laid over the anticipated rising fatigue of the players. Every day had its own practice plan, but you knew to expect an exactitude and that practice would end on time, a certainty that eased the toughness of the hour and forty-five minutes...."[39]

This kind of attention to detail works in the business world, not just in athletics. An orchestrated plan is virtually essential if you are involved in planning special events, advertising campaigns, promotions, and so on.

Whenever a number of people are involved and layered tasks must get done, you had better have a detailed plan of who does what, when, how, and what to do if something goes wrong. If you don't enjoy producing detailed plans, or if you have no talent for it, find someone in the organization who can, or hire someone to do it.

❧

ANTICIPATE TROUBLE

According to one account, Murphy's Law is named for Captain Ed Murphy, who was a development engineer at Wright Field Aircraft Lab in Muroc, California, in the 1940s. Murphy was frustrated because a crucial part had been malfunctioning due to a technician's faulty wiring. "If there is any way to do it wrong, he will," Murphy told George E. Nichols, the quality assurance manager for the project.

Nichols began to refer to the phenomenon as "Murphy's Law." Not long afterward, the director of an Air Force project stated at a press conference that an excellent safety record had been achieved because of a firm belief in "Murphy's Law." The idea was picked up by the press and soon found its way into our national culture.[40]

Some say there wasn't a real Murphy. The so-called law is a facetious way of describing the second law of thermodynamics, which says, essentially, that you can't ever break even because you always must put in more than you get back.

Murphy's Law goes as follows: If anything can go wrong, it will. There are several humorous but telling corollaries to Murphy's Law:

- If there is a possibility of several things going wrong, the one that will go wrong is the one that will embarrass you the most.

- If your attack is going well, you have walked into an ambush.

- If the enemy is in range, so are you.

- It's impossible to make anything foolproof, because fools are so ingenious.

I have proposed an amendment to Murphy's Law. Griessman's amendment is: *Anything can go wrong, so take along a toolkit—and allow yourself time to make the repairs.*

Is this amendment at odds with positive thinking? Not at all. In an imperfect world, imperfection happens. The core wisdom of positive thinking is this: Even though things go wrong, you can turn them around if you are prepared to do so.

That's what Bill Toomey did when he prepared for Olympic competition. His research indicated that it often had rained during past decathlon events. Toomey also noticed that many of his competitors quit practicing when it started raining. So Toomey learned to perform in the rain. Sure enough, in 1968, when he competed in Mexico City, it rained. Toomey told me, "When it started to rain, I couldn't wait to get out there."

And what do you suppose happened? Bill Toomey won the gold. Bill Toomey positioned himself for an unlucky break to occur. Unlucky for the others. Lucky for him. So, don't just save for a rainy day, prepare to compete in it.

Whenever you are embarking on any project, think of all the ways that something can go wrong and try to devise ways to deal with them if they do go wrong. If someone gives you directions to, say, a reception that is being held at a residence in the suburbs, write down the instructions as carefully as possible. If you are told that it will take approximately 30 minutes to reach the location, add a few minutes to your travel time, because you will most certainly make at least one wrong turn, probably several. If you are told, "There's no way to miss it," you *will* miss it.

In the unlikely event that you arrive too early, you can profitably spend the time going over items on your to-do list, doing some serious thinking about priorities and goals, making calls on your car phone, and so on.

There is another example of Murphy's Law and Griessman's amendment: When people tell you how to do something, they will probably omit telling you at least one crucial step. The reason they omit telling you about this crucial step is because this step is so obvious to them, they would never omit doing it themselves. They assume that you wouldn't either. Thus they omit telling you about it. Of course, you won't know to do it because you've never done it before, and they didn't tell you to do it.

Even if you take the precaution to repeat the instructions, they will probably fill in all the gaps with the exception of the most crucial one. So, know how to reach somebody who can help you when you start following instructions. You are not going to be able to do it right the first time and you'll need their help.

There is no better verification of Murphy's Law than when you are learning to use a computer or new software. The manuals— and many instructors—neglect to tell you some simple but fundamental step, the omission of which can wipe out material that took hours, sometimes days, to input. Even if they tell you about the crucial step, they will slide through it so quickly and in such inexplicable jargon that you won't know what to do.

Recently I met a writer of computer and high-tech manuals. This was my first personal experience with such a person. Immediately I understood why manuals are a problem. She was articulate and knowledgeable. Her wit was dazzling. But that was the problem. She was *too* bright. We need clumsy, slightly dense people to write manuals. They can understand our needs.

Until computer manufacturers and software producers cease hiring brilliant people to write their manuals, don't rely on them. Find a teacher to help you, and if that's impossible, find a telephone number so that you can talk to someone directly and ask stupid questions.

Murphy's Law is comprehensive and apparently universal. Knowing this, some skillful tacticians allocate money in their budgets for the inevitable to occur. One of them is Dr. W. Dallas Hall, director of the Clinical Research Center at Emory University School of Medicine. Hall's work involves preparing major proposals for medical research projects, much of it on deadline, and often involving millions of dollars.

Hall told me he expects that key people will be ill the last few days of the project. He expects the photocopying machine to break down at a crucial time. So, he develops backup plans.

At the beginning of a project, an action plan is prepared that is shared with key participants of the project. Initially, the plan contains all vital names, phone numbers, and fax numbers. It's updated regularly. As the deadline approaches, provisions are made for a backup photocopying machine at a satellite office. A call is made to a temporary agency for a skilled medical secretary to be on standby status just in case someone vital is sick those last few days before deadline. Hall pays a retainer fee for that support.

"I'm in a multi-million-dollar business," says Hall. "I can't afford to miss a deadline because the photocopying machine broke or a key person was sick. You plan on that at baseline."

Don Cameron, a general agent in the life insurance industry, learned from an article that astronauts always have a "Plan B." So he decided to do the same. If he's headed to the airport, he has a Plan B ready in case the flight is canceled or delayed. He's prepared with a Plan B if a key appointment is canceled.

Cameron doesn't expect failure. He just expects difficulties on his way to success. Having a Plan B in readiness increases his probability of success.

Hope for the best, but plan for the worst.

🐍

BUILD IN REDUNDANCY

Redundancy is one of the best ways to cope with Murphy's Law. Griessman's amendment tells you to take along a toolkit and allow time to make the repairs. But also take along spare parts.

Former astronaut John Young is a true believer in redundancy. He was the spacecraft commander of Apollo 16. In 1972, Young and fellow astronaut Charles Duke logged 71 hours on the Cayley Plains of the moon.

When I interviewed Young a few months after that stupendous accomplishment, we talked about his feelings of isolation, tens of thousands of miles away from Earth. "You wish there was more redundancy," he told me, "but because of the weight problem, you can't build as many backup components as you'd like. If one of the switches fails, you're there for a long time."

Even if you never take part in a mission as dramatic as a launch to the moon, you can still utilize the redundancy tactic. Take along an extra bulb for your projector if you're going to do audiovisuals. Pack an extra shirt, and not just one tie either—in case you splatter some lovely sauce all over yourself at dinner. Take along extra batteries in your camera case. You hope you won't need them, but you may.

The best engineers anticipate failure by adding backup elements to insure success. Redundancy is a candle in the cupboard, an emergency generator at the hospital if the lights fail, an extra parachute.

If you're staying in a hotel and you have a very important meeting early in the morning, you leave a message for a wake-up call. You also set an alarm clock. If you want breakfast brought to your room before an early appointment, you place the order the night before, and then just as soon as you wake up, you make a second (i.e., redundant) call. The person who took your order the night before may have forgotten. It's just a simple way to take out some insurance.

If you've made an appointment a week in advance to have lunch with somebody, call that morning just to confirm. You probably won't need to. The other person may be very dependable. It's redundant. But do it anyway. You'll probably be happy you did because even the most dependable people sometimes forget or have emergencies.

If you think you might need something, you probably will. So, don't throw it away. Keep it for a while. This doesn't mean that you should become a pack rat. Some people have kept their class notes for decades and never have returned to them even once.

But how many times have you thrown something away, like an address, or phone number, or letter, only to find that you needed it a few days or weeks later? Hence, a bit of redundancy with vital information is an important time tactic. Keep a backup list or file of phone numbers and addresses. I enter all important phone numbers, names, and addresses in my computer file. But I also put names and addresses on the Rolodex if I think those are people that I'll be calling regularly. That's a bit redundant, but it's useful and safe.

I also keep my telephone call-back slips for at least one year. On several occasions, being able to go back through a stack of telephone messages helped me retrieve a phone number I couldn't find anywhere else.

If you use the computer, the words for redundancy are *backup* and *save*. All the manuals emphasize doing backups and every capable computer instructor teaches it. Some even recommend having two backups. If you have only one and you insert the diskette into a computer that's malfunctioning, you may lose your only backup before you know that the computer is malfunctioning.

Many an individual has worked on a document and lost it all when there was a power surge, or the lights went off, or the hard drive crashed, or the software bombed. The rule of thumb is that you save what you are doing every few minutes and you always back up the completed work. You also take a copy to an off-site location. Some experts recommend backing up everything, every day, every week, every month. If you don't, and you lose everything when things crash or bomb, it can spoil your entire afternoon.

One of my college professors, who was a prolific author, always prepared three copies of his manuscripts in progress. One was kept at home, one was kept at the office, and one was kept in his briefcase. That way, if he ever misplaced or lost one, he had two backup copies.

At the time, I thought that practice a bit paranoid, but I have since learned of several authors—Thomas Carlyle, Ralph Ellison, D. H. Lawrence, among others—who lost manuscripts or had them destroyed by fire or stolen. I personally take the precaution of doing each manuscript on a diskette, making a backup, and keeping a printed copy at a separate place off-site. I would not even want to think about the time that would be spent or the psychological cost I would pay if I were to lose a manuscript that was, say, three-fourths finished.

Time management consultant Harold Taylor provides the following redundancy tips for frequent flyers: Always keep emergency cash somewhere other than in your wallet or purse, such as a $100 or a $50 bill. Make a copy of your airline ticket for easier replacement if it's lost or stolen. If you travel overseas, make copies of your passport pages that bear the passport number. Make copies of your credit cards by laying them on the photocopier. (If the embossed numbers don't come out clearly, rub carbon paper over the cards before copying.) Always have a contingency plan in case you miss connections.

Author and consultant Michael Mescon has been making presentations to major companies for years. The other day he told me about an experience he had several years ago when he made a presentation for a large gathering of IBM people at a secluded rural resort in Arkansas. A representative of the company met him at the airport and showed him to his car. As they made their way toward the conference area, Mescon noticed that another car was following them. He asked why. His host replied, "We sent that car in case this one breaks down." When he reached the auditorium, they gave him not one but two mikes. Mescon asked why. "Just in case one of them fails," was the reply.

After Mescon made his presentation, he noticed a distinguished-looking man, who looked somewhat like Colonel Sanders, standing nearby. Mescon asked him if he was on the program. The man replied, "I would have been if you hadn't showed up."

ॐ
PREPARE A SCRIPT

J. B. Fuqua has made a fortune putting deals together. One of his most important tools has been the telephone. Fuqua insists that the ability to talk on the phone should be taught in business schools.

I asked Fuqua how he uses the phone. Here's his reply: "I make simple notes before I call," he replied. "When I get on the phone, I get to the point—I don't talk about the weather—I get the phone call over with, and that's that."

Fuqua uses that same approach for meetings too. "When I talk with people in my office, I try to carry in my mind a reasonable agenda, and if I go to see somebody else, I do the same thing...."

The approach Fuqua is describing can be thought of as a kind of script. The script is developed in terms of objectives, goals, victories to be won. It may be no more than key words and phrases and an objective jotted down on the back of an envelope. A script is like a storyboard that people in advertising use to develop a TV commercial. The storyboard develops the concept by arranging the key ideas in a logical manner.

How do you know what words and phrases to use? Think of all the possible ways the individual on the other end of the line, or across the desk, will react. Then devise appropriate strategies for all the possible reactions. You won't plan everything out, word for word, but you will be prepared to use key words, phrases, and names, while avoiding others.

Help from a coach on the inside of the organization can be useful. Such a person will know if there are some words and names that will annoy—or delight—the other person.

Probably the single most important idea to remember in effective communication is knowing how to package your message. Does the target individual like short communications or long ones? Does that person prefer a written message or an oral one? When you're preparing the script, you need to know.

Fuqua's style is brief and to the point. Very little extraneous socializing is added to the basic objective. But there are many exceptions. Some people enjoy socializing along with their business. They like to mix short chats with a friend along with the business.

There's no hard and fast rule. Getting right to the point may seem blunt and impolite in some settings, even rude. The target individual may appreciate it if you don't rush them. That's certainly true in many countries outside the United States, where it is considered uncivilized and poor business practice to plunge right into business matters. If you start too soon with the sales presentation, you may as well pack your bags. You are not going to sell anything.

Script writing is not easy. But it's better to have a script than to try to wing it. If you don't, you may forget to bring up a vital point, and if the interaction is with someone who's difficult to see, the point may be difficult to bring up again. Without a script, you run the risk of unselling. Successful people in sales know that if you continue to sell *after* a customer has decided to buy, you can unsell them.

A good script tells you what you intend to achieve. And when you have achieved it, say your exit lines.

Having a script doesn't mean that you can't improvise. A script, after all, is a tactic. It is based on your best guess about how the conversation or meeting will go. If there's an unexpected turn, you must be prepared to deal with it.

In fact, the unexpected turn may lead you to a brilliant insight, a startling discovery, a fascinating story. Go with the story. Explore the insight. But if the unexpected turn takes you far from your intended objective, then you will want to try to take control and bring it back as diplomatically as possible.

Whenever I interview for radio, TV, newspapers, or magazines, I always have a list of questions and topics I want to pursue. That list is my script. I create the script by thinking hard about what the individual will be like, what questions I should ask at the beginning to gain their confidence, what topics to bring up and in what order. Several of the items will be musts, others maybes.

Sometimes, in the actual interview, the person I'm interviewing will embark on a long anecdote. If I know the time available is limited, I must decide whether listening to the anecdote will help me get needed information, provide some unexpected insight, or simply waste the available time. I am always willing to adapt to an unexpected turn in the conversation, always keeping in mind what my objectives are. But I will find some way to get in the *must* questions.

Really good people in sales often write down effective ways to say things so that they can use them again. They often will stumble on a way to close or deal with an objection. The good ones profit from the accident, make a note of it, and use it again. That discovery becomes part of the script.

❧ 14 ❧

Use Technology That Works

❧
PHONE TACTICS THAT SAVE TIME

The telephone can be an invaluable part of your time-saving strategy. Think of the telephone as a genie in the bottle. A recent GTE advertisement has a photograph of a telephone, with this message: If Time Is Money, This Is a Bank.

Take a good look at your telephone. Think for a moment about what this instrument can connect you to: enormous databases, all sorts of knowledgeable and interesting individuals, an incalculable range of services. Hook it up to a modem and the list expands exponentially. You can do your grocery shopping, register for classes, check on the availability of a book at the library without leaving your room or office, find out what your bank balance is, purchase an airline ticket, and get the latest stock quotations. And with more high-power technology coming down the pike—like expanded electronic mail, storage of electronic data, the merging of voice and data transmission—the telephone will become even more fabulous.

In order to realize the telephone's vast potential, one of the most important fundamentals involves learning how to get through to key people. (I've done workshops for people, like CEOs, who wanted me to tell them how to avoid unwanted callers. But CEOs need to get through to people too.) Here are some tips from some of the most successful people in the world at doing that:

- *Use a script.* (See preceding chapter for guidelines.)
- *Get to knowledgeables and decision makers as quickly as possible.* Don't waste time with people who can't make decisions unless you are trying to find out who the decision maker is. If you don't have the name of the decision maker, call the switchboard and ask for the name of the person who makes appointments for the president or director of the department. This will usually be the executive secretary or executive assistant. This person will have authority and be knowledgeable as well, and the switchboard operator can tell you who it is. Almost always, I get to a senior and knowledgeable person who will tell me who does what. Often that person will transfer my call to a more appropriate individual. The call then comes in to the next unit from the president's office or the director's office and is unlikely to be ignored.
- *Use people's names when you can.* You may want to make the first call just to get the name of the key gatekeeper and the target individual. Your first call might be an inquiry such as the following: "I'm going to be sending some information to your company. Could I verify the company name, address and so on? I would like to direct this information to the facility manager's (or vice president of sales, vice president of marketing, etc.) attention. Who might that be?" You may want to mail some information or a letter before you call. But when you call the next time, you can ask for your party by name.

  Perhaps the most important name to learn is the name of the receptionist/secretary/assistant of the person you're trying to reach. Headhunter Don Anthony makes a conscious effort to turn the gatekeeper into his own employee. He begins this way:

  DON: Hello, I'm Don Anthony. With whom am I speaking?

  JULIE: Julie.

  DON: Julie, I need your help in getting Terry Mayfield on the phone. It's important that we speak....

Anthony believes that using the gatekeeper's name and asking her to help is crucial in doing his job. "When Julie gets me through to Terry, she's the one who got it done. That can work after I have used her name."

By the simple courtesy of using the gatekeeper's name, Anthony often can initiate other requests. If the gatekeeper refers him to another person, he will sometimes ask, "What kind of person is he?" What he is doing is turning the person who answers the phone into a coach. If he suspects the person who answers the phone is untrained, like a temporary receptionist, Anthony asks the person's name, makes the request, then says: "Julie, I'm someone he will want to speak with."

■ *Anticipate what the gatekeeper will ask before you call.* The gatekeeper is probably going to want your name, the name of your company, and perhaps the nature of your call. A salesperson at a workshop suggested the following opening sentences that can help you sail right past those screening questions: "I'm Tom Bradley with Bradley and Associates. I *need* to speak with John Williams." By answering in advance the two questions most gatekeepers are primed to ask—Who are you? and Who are you with?—and giving your call a sense of urgency ("I *need* to speak to John Williams") you can sometimes get right through.

■ *Don't be stopped by the first block.* Football coaching legend Paul "Bear" Bryant once told me that winning football consists of first and second and third efforts. So, if the person on the other end of the line tells you, "She's in a meeting," or "She's on the phone," don't stop. That's only the first tackle. Her "meeting" may be a chat about politics or gossip about the shenanigans of someone in another office. She might be wrapping up her telephone conversation. The "meeting" could be halted on a moment's notice, and no one would care.

Of course, there are meetings and phone calls that cannot be interrupted. Thus, the tactic that follows should generally be used only if you already have established a relationship with the person you're calling. If you're cold calling, you just may have a very hostile person on the other end of the line when he or she discovers that it is a cold call.

Here's one way to execute this tactic. Begin by pointing out an advantage to the gatekeeper: "So we won't play telephone tag, I wonder if you might help me? Are you where you can slip her a note?" If the answer is yes, then say, "Would you slip her a note and tell her I'll be willing to hold if she would like for me to?" I've discovered that perhaps as often as half the time—if I can get the gatekeeper to agree to slip the person a note—I get through to the person. The gatekeeper will come back on the line with a reply like, "She said if you can hold for another minute, she'll be with you."

The percentages for success drop drastically when you deal with very high-profile people. They simply are harder to reach. But if this tactic results in connecting only 10 percent of your calls, making this request can be a major time-saver.

- *Make telephone appointments.* If the person you want is out or if the meeting is uninterruptible, ask for the best time to try again. Many time tacticians actually make an appointment to call back. Ask, "Can you make appointments for her?" If the answer is yes, say, "I wonder if I could make a telephone appointment? If you'll give me an exact time, I will call precisely at that time." I personally have used this tactic a number of times to end telephone tag.

- *Name-drop.* If possible, be able to say to the gatekeeper, "Tell her Tom Brooks, the president of Provident Finance, asked me to call." There's a bit of a risk in this because, without your knowing it, Tom Brooks may be detested by the person that you are calling. But if you're pretty sure that Tom Brooks is a respected name, by all means use it. Better still, ask Tom Brooks to set up your call by calling ahead or having his assistant do so.

- *Intrigue them in order to get them to call back.* Don Anthony has discovered a simple sentence that causes people to return his calls most of the time. He says it's magic the way this message works: "Julie, would you please leave this message for Tom? Tell him that *I have something interesting to share with him.*" Anthony says people can't seem to resist this message. Their curiosity makes them call to find out what the interesting information is. He adds, "Of course, you had better have something interesting to share when Terry does return the call."

- *Create telephone relationships.* Katrina Dinkle, one of the nation's top institutional bond salespersons, has never met some of her very best customers face-to-face. She's dealt with some of them for years and done millions of dollars of transactions with them over the phone. She admitted that now she's a little bit nervous about actually seeing them because she is afraid an in-person meeting might break the spell and destroy the magic the phone has made possible.

  For many situations, avoid in-person meetings. They can be time-wasters. Use the phone. As obvious as this idea seems, some people insist on holding a meeting when a phone call can work just as well, or maybe better.

- *Call early. Call late.* Gatekeepers can be deadly. An officious gatekeeper can thwart the most skillful assault. But gatekeepers often arrive at nine and leave at five, and they often take full-length lunches. Decision makers tend to come early and/or stay late and they often have lunch brought in. So the best time to get to Mr. or Ms. Decision Maker may be when the gatekeepers are not around. That may be early in the morning or late in the afternoon or evening. I know one top salesperson who will cold call between 7 and 8 a.m., during lunch, and after 5:30 p.m. Often it's the decision maker who picks up the phone because the gatekeeper isn't in.

- *Use speakerphones and conference calls.* This enables several people to exchange information and perhaps come to a decision. Otherwise, you may have to make several individual phone calls. However, don't use a speakerphone for one-on-one calls. It may be time-efficient, but many people resent it. One effective way you can use a speakerphone is when you're on hold. You can do other work, open mail, do paperwork, and so on, until you hear the other party pick up. That may be several minutes later, so it can be a great time-saver. One CEO I know uses a headphone to accomplish the same purpose. He loves it. The headphone enables him to walk around the office and do other chores while he's on the phone, whether he's on hold or not.

- *In some instances, it is advantageous to be the caller, not the callee.* Everybody knows that there are times when you want to be the one sought. You won't want to seem too interested in getting the job or too anxious to sell. That may weaken your bargaining position. But there are distinct advantages for the person who makes the call. The caller can think in advance what to say. The caller can have needed reference material close at hand and—if they follow the advice in this book—a script. The person being called, by contrast, may be caught off-guard, in the middle of something else, and may not have the needed information readily available.

- *Obtain and record the number for the direct line to anyone you need to call again.* This vital piece of information can get you past the gatekeeper. Also, you'll be able to get past the main switchboard after-hours. Request the number the first time you get through.

- *Return the phone call as quickly as possible.* Some individuals allocate certain times of the day or week for returning calls. That way, they aren't constantly interrupted and distracted. However, this practice will increase the amount of time that you spend playing telephone tag. Why? Because the person may not be there to accept the return call at the block of time that you have allocated for the task. The best time to catch callers is immediately after they call. If you wait very long, the caller may leave the office or become involved in doing something that can't be interrupted.

  If you return phone calls immediately, people like it. They resent not having calls returned. Some individuals resent it a lot. College president Johnnetta Cole told me: "I think it is not only an expression of business etiquette, I think it's an expression of human decency. If someone has called you, they didn't just randomly say, 'What shall I do today?'"

  The longer you wait to return the call, the more likely the caller is to think bad thoughts about you. Returning phone calls immediately is a discipline that makes you more efficient. If you return calls immediately, they don't add up. You don't have a huge block of calls that you have to fight your way through. And phone calls can be returned immediately. If you're in a meeting, return them when you're out of the meeting. If you're traveling, return them from the road, from an airplane, when you're changing planes.

- *Be interruptible.*   When I checked my voice mail recently, there was a message from Tom Hussey, a successful stockbroker in Savannah. Hussey wasn't calling to try to sell me anything. He was calling to see if I would be available to do a public seminar in that city. Here is the message I heard: "Hi, This is Tom Hussey. Please call me right away. *If I'm on the phone, please have me interrupted.*"

The last sentence of his message is a powerful time tactic. Let me explain why. For years, I've been teaching people that they should be interruptible. Obviously, there are times when you absolutely do not want anything to interrupt you. But there are other instances when you can miss a truly important call because you are doing something that could easily be continued later.

I have taught my assistants to let me know when calls come in by slipping me a note. We have a little arrangement whereby I will look at the name on the note. If I'm on the phone, I'll hold up one finger or two. One finger means that I can be off the phone in just a moment. "Request them to stay on the line." Two fingers means that the present call will probably take quite a while to complete. The assistant knows to ask when will be a good time for me to call back.

Several years ago a U.S. senator, whom I had been trying to reach for an important interview for weeks, finally called. I happened to be on the phone at the time, and the secretary who answered told his office to call back later. "He's on the phone," she told them. It took almost forever to get the interview because I missed his returned call.

Tom Hussey made use of the tactic as diplomatically and as persuasively as I've ever heard. In fact, I now use Hussey's phraseology myself. I leave word, "If I'm on the phone, please have me interrupted."

The tactic is efficient. It eliminates some of the time you spend playing telephone tag. It implements your priorities. All phone calls are not created equal. Some information is more urgent than others.

But the main reason the tactic works is because it signals to the receiver that you consider that person important enough to interrupt whatever you are doing to take the call. That's a powerful message to send.

It's not often that you can be efficient and pay someone a compliment at the same time.

- *Purchase a mobile phone or a car phone.* For many people, the car phone has become a necessity. It is such a great time-saver. You can have calls forwarded to your car. You can return calls immediately by checking your voice mail. You can use it to dictate messages to your assistant. If you're lost, you can call for directions. If you're running late, you can call to inform the other party what's happening. If your car breaks down, you can summon help and avoid danger.

Auto-leasing expert Dick Biggs uses his car phone primarily to communicate short messages, not for calls that may run long. It's too expensive presently for that, he says. But Biggs uses a car phone continually for setting or altering appointments (in case of traffic tie-ups), picking up messages, and so on.

"A car phone's like a microwave," a successful sales manager told me. "You don't think you really need one, but once you get it, you use it all the time—and wonder how you ever got along without one." Marketing guru Alf Nucifora uses a car phone to create the "chunks" of time mentioned earlier. He gathers up all his phone messages and returns them on his car phone when he's traveling to meetings and appointments.

In some occupations and some locations, a portable phone has advantages over a car phone. Without one, an architect or an engineer in the field might be inaccessible for extended periods of time and miss vital messages. With a portable phone, you can make important calls from the cab, on the way to the airport in the limousine, or when all the phones are tied up at the airport.

Communications consultant and trainer Ken Futch finds his portable phone invaluable at a conference. Generally at the breaks between sessions, usually every phone will be in use. Futch uses his portable phone to avoid the lines.

- *Go for quality features and options.* Nothing is more irritating than a phone call that sounds tiny or indistinct. Pay the few extra dollars to get a smart phone that sounds good and has such functions as special numbers for storing frequently called phone numbers and a redial.

■ *Don't be greedy.*   Generally it's best to place your own calls. It may be cost-efficient to let someone who earns less than you do make your calls, but people often resent it. You can get away with having someone else place your calls if you're the boss calling a subordinate; if you're the buyer, not the seller; if you're the President; or if you're sure that the person called will be absolutely thrilled just to have you phone them. But I know of no telephone practice more likely to make people dislike you than to have someone place your calls and then expect the person called to wait until you get on the line. You are sending a clear signal to the person being called, "My time is more valuable than yours."

The treasurer of a major airline told me that he recently had a phone call from a secretary who said to him, "Would you please hold for Mr. Blank?" He replied, "I'll hold for five seconds." Mr. Blank wasn't on the line in five seconds and he hung up. The president of a design firm in New York City told me about a vendor who has his secretary place his calls to potential customers. "I will never buy anything from him," the president stated with some irritation, just remembering the event. "Can you believe it? He's trying to sell me something, and he expects me to wait for him to get on the line."

If you think your time is more valuable than the other person's, and you don't mind saying this loud and clear, go ahead and do it. If not, make the call yourself.

■ *Use a fax to break out of a telephone-tag cycle.*   If you've been going back and forth, send the person a fax. Fax messages tend to be read immediately. You may be able to say everything with the fax.

MAKE THE MOST OF VOICE MAIL

Some people hate voice mail. Some people love it. How you feel about it depends on what your needs are and how well you use it.

Used correctly, voice mail can eliminate errors in communication and save time in dozens of ways. With voice mail, it's no longer necessary to talk in real time. Sometimes a voice message will do the job quicker and better than actually speaking to someone directly. Whenever I want to leave a message for someone I know, and that person isn't in, I often ask their administrative assistant or secretary if I can leave the message on voice mail. That way I know that errors won't creep in and the message won't be filtered through someone else's mind.

I follow the same tactic with answering services. Instead of trying to leave a message with the live person who answers and risk having it garbled, I ask if I can leave a voice message. That way, I can put my own spin on it.

It's not always necessary or desirable to communicate in real time. One executive I know told me that he sometimes deliberately tries to call when the other party is likely to be out in order to leave a short message. If the person is there, he knows the call will usually take longer. I talk with one of my colleagues several times a day, leaving messages in her voice mailbox. She replies promptly to my voice mailbox, without either of us having to wait for the other to come to the phone or get off the phone with someone else.

Recently the president of a large company told me that he hated voice mail. Actually, he said he "despised" it. When he told me how he used voice mail, I understood why. He didn't leave completed messages. He was just leaving call-back messages.

I told him to think of voice mail as a substitute for writing a letter. Anything that he can do in a letter, he can do with voice mail. I suggested that in the future he leave a voice letter, not just his name.

Voice mail can be used to screen calls. If you're hiring, you can use it to take applications. Voice-mail packages are available to take verbal résumés, so that the applicant fills out the form orally. Voice mail can also be used to give priorities to your messages. Douglas Chance of Octel Communications uses a feature called nonsimultaneous communications. Outsiders can reach him directly by phone, but employees use the voice-mail system unless there's an emergency. Chance returns employees' messages at his convenience.

Voice mail can be used to give directions and store hours. Several companies are in the business of creating professional customized messages. Some voice-mail systems have the ability to store faxes and forward them. If you have this option, you can send a fax into your system with, say, the specifications for one of your products or a description of your programs. Once it is stored, you can then send it to any number of fax machines.

One important caution if you are installing a voice-mail system. Don't have a long menu up front that the caller must work through. At most, have three or four options. If it's too long and complicated, the caller will become annoyed and hang up.

Most voice-mail systems have a mechanism to get you to a real person, usually by dialing 0 or by holding. This option is built into most systems because rotary phones are still in use. Occasionally companies will program the voice mail to let nobody through unless they know a code or extension number, but that's rare. If you've been frustrated by voice mail because you can't get through to a person, just remember that you can usually bail out of voice mail and get to one. Then you use the phone strategies mentioned above.

ॐ
WHEN POSSIBLE, AUTOMATE

Routine tasks can be handled by technology. Let your employer deposit your check for you. There's no point in physically taking your check to the bank and depositing it yourself. Use automatic pay for utility bills and any other companies that will allow you to use that service. Consider purchasing a computer program that will do this service for you, like the Peachtree Business Checkbook or Quicken.

Purchase a fax if you don't already own one. Even if you use it just for social purposes, the amount of time it can save will amaze you. And be sure to get one with features like automatic paper cutters and feeders, speed dialing, and redial.

In some situations, a beeper, or pager, can be a real time-saver. Professional and businesspeople have used beepers for years in order to keep in touch with their offices when they have to be away from a phone. Many actors carry them so that they won't miss opportunities for auditions when their agents call. The beeper is catching on as a short-term convenience for a wider range of needs. They can now be rented on a daily or a weekly basis in many locations.

Owning your own copier may be a wise choice. Don't skimp on features and quality if you do.

Technology can make work for you or against you. You can be overwhelmed by electronic mail. When John Whiteside, a software engineer at Digital Equipment Corporation, returned from a three-week assignment, his computer screen showed that he had literally hundreds of electronic messages waiting for him.

Which ones should he read first, and which not at all? Whiteside solved that technology problem by developing some new technology. He programmed his computer to assign each incoming message a code that identifies the sender. A message from his manager or vice president or president goes into a high-priority electronic file. Announcements about cafeteria hours go at the bottom.[41]

There is no ultimate solution. Every "solution" creates a new problem, which in turn requires a new solution. Anthropologists disagree about which was the first human solution. Some say it was a weapon; others, language; still others, fire. Whichever came first, each solution is also a problem.

Sometimes what seems to be a solution isn't one at all, not even short-term. Many companies overuse computers and advanced technology. They, in effect, use cannons to kill mice. The time and resources needed to install, learn, and use many technologies far outweigh any possible benefit that could be derived from them.

That risk notwithstanding, look for a handy tool to use whenever you do anything repetitive, big, or dangerous. Take to heart an IBM slogan: Machines should work. People should think.

&

THE TIME-SAVING USES OF COMPUTER TECHNOLOGY

Revolutions have accompanied three great events in the history of communication. The first communication revolution accompanied the invention of writing. The second revolution occurred many thousands of years later when movable type was created by Gutenberg in the fifteenth century.

The third great communication revolution has occurred only recently with the advent of electricity-based communication technologies, such as telegraph, telephone, the phonograph, radio, TV, and tape recording. This revolution is still under way, with the early electricity-based technologies now becoming merged by the computer. Information can be transmitted, received, stored, and retrieved almost instantly. What is known as "massively parallel computing" is measured in *gigaflops*. (A gigaflop is 1 billion floating-point operations per second.) The last time I checked, the world record was 5.2 gigaflops, but it may be far faster than that by the time you read this book. Obviously, you can print a lot of messages, access a lot of messages, transmit a lot of messages with technology this powerful and this fast.

What are the implications for you? It can enlarge your territory. You can access the world, even if you are a one-person operation—with a computer and a modem. It can expand your intellectual horizons. It can make learning easier, more efficient, and more fun. The day is almost here when you can walk into a public library and get all the information copied on a disk that you don't have to return. No, let me correct that. You won't have to walk to the library. You can send for the information via modem. It can break down social barriers. A poor teenager who is computer savvy, regardless of color or religion or national origins, can know more than rich elders.

New ways to solve problems are now possible, thanks to the computer. Boeing's new 777 will be the world's first paperless plane. It will be designed entirely on the computer using CAD/CAM technology and 3-D capabilities.

The downside of this capacity is information overload. It's impossible to keep up with everything that is out there. We also are vulnerable to disruptions caused by outages, terrorism, or natural disasters.

Here are a few ways to make the computer your faithful, hard-working friend:

- *Use the computer to assist with your research.* We used to have to plod manually through big reference books and guides to periodical literature, concordances, and the like. These were books and periodicals that you had to physically work through. Today many reference aids are computer-accessible. Searches can be conducted simply by typing in a word or name.

- *Use the computer to calculate and do your spreadsheets.* Accounting packages, bookkeeping systems, and tax preparation software all can make your recordkeeping go smoother. Financial analysis software, market forecasting programs, and powerful spreadsheet packages can provide insight and help to avoid costly mistakes. The best systems will take you through step by step and show you how to use them. Time-saving benefits include instant calculations, meaningful graphs, and stunning presentations.

- *Use the computer to track customers and clients.* Several off-the-shelf software packages, like Telemagic and ACT, are available at low cost that will enable you to keep up with all your interactions with customers and clients.

- *Use the computer to store and to retrieve.* File away all sorts of information that you create, and access information on virtually any subject through the numerous databases that are now available.

- *Use the computer to communicate.* One of the excellent options available to many computer users is computer mail. Instead of writing a letter or a note and putting it in the mail, the user simply types the message into the computer and sends it electronically to receivers' "mailboxes." A naval officer who attended one of my workshops shared this time tactic with the group: "I communicate all nonessential information, replies, and the like to my supervisor and employees through the use of computer mail. This now takes only a few minutes to contact some 20 people. I used to call or write letters and spent in excess of an hour."

- *Use the computer to do routine tasks.* The computer can address your envelopes and make out your checks.

- *Use the computer to help you organize your life.* College president Johnnetta Cole told me that she is astonished at the ways her portable electronic organizer helps her. She uses it to record her appointments and memos as well as store important phone numbers and addresses.

Here are some guidelines to follow when using a computer:

- *Become computer literate.* It doesn't take much time to learn the basics. Take a short course, rent or purchase a video, or hire a tutor.

  And learn how to touch-type. You may be able to get by with a hunt-and-peck system, but if you will take the time to learn to touch-type, you'll be hours ahead. The heart of a computer keyboard is a typewriter keyboard, so if you can touch-type accurately and rapidly, it increases your computer competence.

  Professional speaker Barbara Pagano remembers a confrontation her mother had with her high school counselor. Her counselor wouldn't let her enroll in a course called "business typing" because she was on the "college-bound" course of study. Pagano remembers the last words her mother said to the counselor: "She *will* take business typing." And she did.

  Pagano told me, "It was the best move I ever made. I got summer jobs for big bucks while my friends were working at low-paying ones. And it continues to pay off, now that I use the computer."

  That's been my experience, too. The very first course I took in college was a typing course. For years I've urged university students to take typing, but I'm not sure that you can do that now at many colleges and universities. I suppose touch-typing seems too elementary, perhaps too practical to find a place in the modern curriculum. But it's no longer necessary to take a course. The computer can teach you. Several inexpensive tutorial software packages are available that will enable you to teach yourself.

Even if you go to the highest position in a company, you still are certain to encounter situations in which you will need to deal with a computer keyboard. Knowing how to use it efficiently will be an enormous time-saver.

After you've acquired the basic skills, you may want to take courses in advanced computer techniques, like learning how to create a spreadsheet or how to make a storyboard for a presentation.

- *Know how to find help.* Your first resort may be the help line of the software or hardware company. Another is to have a friend or tutor whom you can call. Finally, knowing someone who's knowledgeable at a computer store can be an invaluable resource.

- *Find out what's available.* Periodically browse in a well-stocked computer store or look through a computer catalog or read one of the many computer magazines periodically. You'll probably be amazed at what's available.

- *Use on-line resources like CompuServe or Prodigy.* For a modest monthly fee, you will have access to travel guides, movie reviews, current stock reports, restaurant reviews, and weather reports from all over the world. You will be able to order groceries, airline tickets, and mutual funds from your computer. And if you need specific information, you can post your request on a bulletin board.

When computer expert Terry Brock traveled to Dubai recently, he asked for up-to-date information on that part of the world through his CompuServe bulletin board. Within a matter of hours he received numerous messages with all sorts of information about what to do, where to go, and what to avoid. During the Gulf War, a woman in Washington State posted a note on the food and wine bulletin board asking for recipes for cookies that would survive the trip to the Gulf. Not only did the woman receive recipes, but she received several offers from Prodigy users to actually bake the cookies.

Marketing expert Don Peppers likes to tell about a national quilt auction that recently took place in a midwestern town. The quilts of one group of women continually fetched the highest prices. Those women actually lived in different parts of the county but shared quilting patterns back and forth by computer, on the Prodigy network. "They were from all over the country, and they were friends."[42] Peppers calls such groups "image tribes."

BECOME AN EFFECTIVE DICTATOR

One reason acclaimed historian Mel Kranzberg has been able to carry on extensive correspondence with colleagues, friends, and research collaborators all over the world is his skill at using dictating equipment. He is able to produce enormous amounts of work. Moreover, his writing has that wonderful quality of sounding as though he is communicating directly with you, as though he were talking with you.

Zig Ziglar carries a tape recorder with him everywhere. As soon as he gets into a car, he pops in a tape. When he's driving along, if he hears an idea that stimulates a thought, he cuts off the tape that he's listening to and dictates the idea on his portable dictation unit.

Research shows that people on the average can write approximately 20 words per minute, which means that a letter with 185 words takes over 9 minutes to write. Dictating the same 185 word letter takes only 2½ minutes, saving you approximately 6 minutes.

If you produce three to five documents a day by dictation, you will save up to 30 minutes a day. Now look at the chart at the beginning of the book to see how much 30 minutes a day is worth in dollars and cents. If you earn $50,000 per year, and you save half an hour a day producing written material, you have saved over $12 per day. If you do that for a year, one-half hour saved a day comes to $3125. (The time spent transcribing from tape to printed page is approximately the same as time spent deciphering handwritten copy, perhaps less. So the transcribing time is a wash.)

Many very efficient people use dictating equipment not simply to write letters and manuscripts but to leave instructions for their assistants and secretaries. I've been following this practice for years. It has the advantage of being a quick way of giving instructions. Additionally, a recorded message provides the benefit of easy review. My assistant or secretary can replay the tape to make sure that the communication is correct. That isn't possible with verbal instructions. (Granted, the assistant could reread *written* instructions.) However, because I can dictate the instruction more rapidly and explain it by using illustrations and saying it two or three different ways, I can build in the redundancy necessary to make sure that the communication is clear.

Be sure not to skimp on quality when you purchase dictating equipment. You can do your dictating with an inexpensive recorder. But you'll be able to do it much more efficiently and pleasantly if you will spend a few more dollars and purchase a piece of equipment that's made specifically for dictating (e.g., with one-finger controls and other dictating functions).

You may already have a piece of dictating equipment and don't know it. It's your answering machine or voice mail. Use it to dictate short notes or memos, or even letters if its time limit isn't too restrictive. Your assistant can pop out the cassette from the answering machine and load it into the transcribing machine. Many voice-mail systems have procedures for downloading or dubbing to a transcribing unit.

I know of a few exceptions to this tactic. One president of a large international food distributor told me that he prefers to dictate in person rather than use a machine. He says he likes to watch his secretary's reaction to his ideas. "I like to see her eyes light up," he says. He's willing to give up some time efficiency in order to get the feedback.

One other negative observation on the tactic. If you've been used to writing out everything, you will be much less efficient while you learn how to master dictating technique. But it's worth it. Dictators get their work done quickly, efficiently, and pleasantly.

❧ 15 ❧

Balancing Work,
Family,
and Social Life

❧

IF I'M SO EFFICIENT, WHY AM I SO
MISERABLE?

Modern man thinks he loses something—time—when he does not do things quickly, yet he does not know what to do with the time he gains except kill it. —ERIC FROMM

Why is there is so much unhappiness in Western civilization—despite its abundance? The abundance is part of the problem. Psychologist B. F. Skinner believed that profusion can make us bored and weak. "People look at beautiful things, listen to beautiful music, and watch exciting entertainments," Skinner observed, "but the only behavior reinforced is looking, listening, and watching."

In leaner times in history, this was not a problem. Few good choices were available to most people. Careers were severely restricted, entertainment was limited, and marriages were often arranged. Most people grew up, married, had a family, worked, worshipped, and died within well-worn grooves.

The United States with its vast frontiers and its belief in personal freedom produced an opportunity for people to live anywhere, do anything, fail and start over again doing something different if they wanted to. As a result, Americans are a restless people, and have been for a long time. Alexis de Tocqueville, a French nobleman, observed in the 1830s: "In the United States a man builds a house in which to spend his old age, and he sells it before the roof is on, he plants a garden and lets it, just as the trees are coming into bearing....He embraces a profession and gives it up; he settles in a place, which he soon afterwards leaves to carry his changeable longings elsewhere...."[43]

The choices that produced this restlessness in the 1830s have increased dramatically since then. Today, there are an astonishing number of things to do and places to go. Americans are confronted, not by choices between good and bad, but by hundreds of choices among options that are all good. On a given night, an individual might read a book or magazine, attend a night class, listen to a CD, watch a movie, exercise, learn a new language or software, paint, start a business, write, visit with friends or relatives, attend a concert or play, or watch TV. Even watching TV can be a problem. With scores of TV channels to choose from, many viewers cannot enjoy the program on the screen for fear they are missing something better on another channel. So they "surf" with the remote control. TV is watched with the finger, not the eyes.

Partly, the motivation is a thirst for knowledge, for new experience. There is so much to learn and experience, and so little time to do it in. But a virtue becomes a vice when it is exaggerated. You can become so eager to experience something new that you do not enjoy what you have. You can become so excited about reaching your destination that you do not enjoy the views of the journey or the companionship of your fellow travelers.

So, if you wish to achieve balance, do not become overwhelmed by the abundance of your choices. Do not become miserable over what you are *not* doing. Find enjoyment in what you *are* doing, and in who you are, where you are—now.

> Look to this day.
>
> For yesterday is but a dream
>
> And tomorrow only a vision.

But today well lived

Makes every yesterday a dream of happiness

And every tomorrow a vision of hope.

Look well therefore to this day.

—SANSKRIT PROVERB

MAKE AN APPOINTMENT WITH YOURSELF

A great man is coming to eat at my house. I do not wish to please him; I wish that he should wish to please me. —RALPH WALDO EMERSON[44]

The first section of this book briefly described how high achievers organize their daily schedules. Let's return to that idea now, because it is one of the most important ways to bring balance to your life. If you've read the book to this point, you're probably the kind of person who keeps an appointment if you make it. I'd like to recommend that you begin to make appointments with yourself. That's right, put yourself on your appointment schedule. The reason I urge this is because people who have attended my workshops say this is one of the most helpful tactics they've learned.

You already know that this is a great tactic for doing job-related tasks. But consider using it for some dream that you have, like writing a novel or learning some new skill or hobby. But be sure to give it a specific date and time. Paul Oreffice, former CEO of Dow Chemical, puts a tennis match or handball on the list every day, even when he travels. And he puts an extended vacation with his family on his list every year.

Why should you always leave yourself prey to external events? Why should you allocate to yourself only the time that nobody else wants?

Unwillingness to make and keep appointments with yourself may reveal latent feelings of inferiority about yourself. Or it may come from exaggerated courtesy that's self-destructive. Perhaps you feel that everybody else is more important than yourself. If they want your time, they get first claim on it. Why should that be? Banish from your life the idea that everybody takes precedence over you.

Be a friend to yourself. In fact, love yourself. The great commandment "Thou shalt love thy neighbor as thyself" presumes that you love yourself. For if you do not love yourself, how will you know how to love your neighbor?

Don't be the slave of other people's ideas, other people's goals. Don't feel duty-bound to put into your appointment book only what someone else assigns you. And do not be content with leftovers. Give yourself some prime time. Plan to do something for yourself on a regular basis. Just to make sure that it gets done, ink it in with a date and hour.

Putting yourself on your calendar means saying no to other's claims on your time. Highly successful people learn how to protect themselves from people, events, and things that they perceive not to be in their best interest. Their defenses are formidable. They are able to say no, and once they have said it, they dig in their heels. They listen, often very attentively but usually briefly, process the information—you can almost see the wheels turning—and then they decide.

Once you have put yourself on your calendar, you must protect the appointment. Kay Koplovitz's business is TV, which goes on 24 hours a day, 7 days a week. Because there is always some potential claim on her time, she believes that she must have an attitude that protects her time: "If you want to go out and play tennis with some friends at 6:00 on Wednesday, you must protect it as though it's another appointment. In your mind, it is not something to cancel."

❧
TAKE CARE OF YOUR BODY

Over and over again highly successful people mention exercise routines. I have heard it so often that I have come to expect it. Kay Koplovitz has been exercising regularly for 25 years.

Koplovitz prefers the afternoon to the morning and a club rather than a solitary jog or walk. Three times a week she stops at the club and exercises for an hour or so. John Harding, president of National Life of Vermont, gets up at five or six in the morning and works out. Larry King does a treadmill 30 minutes every morning. King says he wasn't an exerciser until his heart surgery six years ago. Now it's automatic. Johnnetta Cole does an early morning 4-mile walk. She calls it her *mobile meditation.*

When Cole first became college president, she didn't schedule exercise as a regular event. She would say to herself: "Oh, there's just so much work to be done. Why don't I just keep pressing on with the work and I'll give up the exercise today." Not anymore. It's a conscious decision. "There are times when I walk with my earphones and I'm listening to my favorite music. There are other times when I don't want to hear anything, except the natural sounds around me, or when I want to even hear my own body in the sense of listening to myself."

Why is exercise so important to these highly successful people? Zig Ziglar has discovered that it helps him write better. Zig Ziglar, who was writing *Over the Top* at the time I interviewed him told me: "Invariably, as I've been writing my book, when I would hit a snag, I would get up, put on my walking shoes and go for a long walk. And invariably, I came back with the answer. Now that didn't happen once. That happened during the course of the book a minimum of 30 times and it could have been 50 times."

John Harding does some of his best creative thinking while he's exercising. Designer Karen Gold while jogging listens to books on tape that she would not otherwise read. Johnnetta Cole says the brisk morning walk energizes her, "clears the head." Kay Koplovitz says her afternoon exercise is "the way I get rid of the tensions and the frustrations that have built up during the day."

The benefits of exercise are mental, emotional, and spiritual. Exercise also happens to be good for the body, too. If you are healthier and have more stamina, you can work better and longer. That by itself is a time tactic, for it enables you to get more out of your day.

High levels of energy is one of the factors that was mentioned by several highly successful people in my interviews for my book *The Achievement Factors*. When I asked renowned architect

Hugh Stubbins what had contributed most to his career, he replied, "energy." Nobel laureate Francis Crick, who is best known for his research on DNA, told me: "One of the things people haven't stressed perhaps enough is, you need a lot of mental energy, or energy of some sort to do all this. It is quite clear that people who are good are not only sort of exuberant—but are also indefatigable. They have really got an enormous capacity to go on doing things for a long time. If you read accounts of (Sir Isaac) Newton, for example, it is clear that he just kept at it and at it and at it."

When I asked Larry King how he managed to keep up with a schedule that includes a daily radio talk show in the afternoon to over 500 stations, and an evening TV show that reaches millions of viewers, plus numerous speaking engagements and celebrity appearances, here's what he replied: "I've always had high energy levels. I never in my life was an eight-hour sleeper. My brother sleeps a long time—sometimes 10 hours. I don't think I've ever slept 10 hours in my life."

But King exercises daily, and he watches his weight and his diet. He takes lots of vitamins. He avoids heavy, fatty foods, eats no cheese, no butter, no eggs, and drinks only skim milk. He does drink coffee, but he never drinks alcohol.

Obviously, metabolism rates, sleep needs, and other factors that contribute to energy levels vary from individual to individual. Whatever your present level is, you can build up your strength through exercising and eating and drinking properly. Neglecting your body is like a city that neglects or abuses its bridges, tunnels, and streets. Sooner or later, what is neglected or abused breaks. If you don't take care of your body, where do you plan to get another one to work and play in?

DO ADD-ONS

Add-ons are a variation of the piggyback tactic. This is one of the least expensive yet best tactics for achieving balance. I know scores of people whose business responsibilities regularly take them to fascinating places in the world. Yet they see nothing of those places except the airport, the highway into town, the hotel they stay in, and the rooms where the meetings are held. Often, with just a bit of planning and a few extra dollars, they could do add-ons by arriving early or staying over for an extra day of life-enriching experiences.

Don't consider such excursions a frivolous waste of time. Consider it part of your lifelong personal enrichment program. That's what the head of the Fulbright program told me when I was a visiting professor in Pakistan, supported by a Fulbright grant. "Obviously we want our professors to do a good job teaching in the nations where they are assigned," he told me one evening over dinner. "But that's not all we want. We want people like you to travel widely, immerse yourself in the culture, learn everything you can, so that when you come back to the States, you'll be more qualified than ever. Our university professors are a national treasure. The more they are enriched, the richer the nation becomes."

Ken Futch regularly schedules vacations for his entire family around his own business schedule. The family likes to ski, so when Futch gets an assignment, say, in Denver, they join him. His own travel and lodging expenses are paid by the client. By paying for his family's transportation and a slight additional hotel cost, Futch enjoys a subsidized vacation. Because he flies a great deal in his regular work, he has built up a bank of frequent-flyer miles that he dips into when he wants to take the family along.

Some time tacticians do weekend layovers. Often family members or a friend will join them. There are numerous advantages. Airline fares are cheaper if a weekend layover is included, and many hotels offer weekend specials, as do rental car companies. It's a great time to get out and enjoy the place you're in. Many people who travel for their work create a collection of guide books and articles plus notes from personal recommendations about the places they go to. One frequent traveler always tries to find out what the best small museum and the best restaurant is in the city she's visiting.

I recently heard of a management consultant—an avid golfer—who does layover golf. Recently he found himself with a long layover at Chicago's O'Hare. He caught a cab to a driving range, hit for an hour, got back in the cab, and made his flight. He improved his swing and reduced his stress.

You can nourish your social life through the same add-on principle. Consider joining some organization that you don't absolutely have to join. You will want to make the choice very carefully, because many organizations are great time-wasters. But civic and church groups and charitable organizations are always looking for dependable and capable members who will take on leadership and committee responsibilities. Often these memberships afford career-enhancing contacts as well as enjoyable social relationships.

LEARN TO LET OTHER PEOPLE HELP YOU

I asked the late W. Edwards Deming, "On a scale of 1 to 10, how time-*conscious* are you?" The founder of the quality movement replied: "That's all I think about."

"How good are you at time *management*, on a scale of 1 to 10?"

"About a 1," Deming answered. (A 10 is excellent; 1 is poor.)

"Then, how do you manage to get so much done?"

Deming's answer: "Sheer luck and help from lots of people."

That's a modest answer, but it contains much truth. Many highly successful people are lucky. And many owe their success to help from lots of people.

The alternative to getting other people to help you is *workaholism*. "I am not a workaholic," Home Depot CEO Bernie Marcus told me. "I don't believe in it. I think it's stupid. I think that these people who come in at five in the morning and go through all the mail, and leave at ten at night with their briefcase are very sad people. I may be insulting a lot of people, but that's the way I feel."

Many of the highly successful people told me they used carefully chosen people to protect them from time-stealing activities and time thieves. They spend time training their assistants so that they understand what their supervisors' priorities are and how certain requests are to be dealt with.

Here's the way Kay Koplovitz described the tactic: "It's really helpful if you have someone capable of prescreening and setting up some priorities. Otherwise, you will just be inundated with tonnage, a lot of which you won't do anything with except discard."

Highly effective people empower their assistants. But they train them, too.

If you are absolutely overwhelmed with things to do, one excellent alternative is to let go of some of it. Perhaps some of it should not be done at all—a tactic already discussed. Other tasks should be done by others. Bernie Marcus believes the people who are forever at the job are basically insecure. "I think they are afraid to let anybody else do any decision making, and they think they are one-of-a-kind. We find that we are not indispensable. Nobody's indispensable. I have tried to make myself dispensable."

ॐ
TAKE A SABBATICAL

The idea of a *sabbath*—a day set aside for rest and religious observance—is an ancient concept that's found in many religious traditions. Sabbaticals have long been used in universities to provide opportunities for scholars to get away and gain new insights. Sabbaticals have begun to take hold in the business world as well.

Many therapists believe that taking a definable break from a work routine can have major benefits for mental and physical health. Think of a sabbatical as a long discretionary chunk of time, the kind Peter Drucker recommends that managers create. Alan Loy McGinnis, a psychotherapist and author of the book *The Power of Optimism,* says we need such openings in our calendar to provide variety in our life rhythm.[45]

McGinnis states that at one time in his own life, he found himself writing too many articles, giving too many speeches, seeing too many patients. So, he took a sabbatical. He laid bricks, planted trees, built cabinets, took long walks, spent time with his grandson. He memorized poetry, spoke Spanish, mastered a computer program, and hiked in the Sierras.

The result? His cholesterol dropped 100 points and his blood pressure 30 points. He felt good physically for the first time in years. His family seemed closer. And when he began to see patients again, he says, "The film was off my eyes."

Another high-profile sabbatical taker is the former Secretary of the U.S. Office of Education Lamar Alexander. In 1988, Alexander booked passage on a cargo ship from California to Australia with his friend, the late Alex Haley, author of *Roots*, for a six-month stepping back from his former life. During that voyage, Alexander wrote a chronicle of the experience entitled *Six Months Off*.

Lisa Shaw, an executive with the Coca-Cola Company, believes that one three-week vacation is much better than three one-week vacations. "One week isn't long enough to change the rhythm," she says. "When I take three weeks, I come back to my job with an entirely new perspective."

Barbara Pagano turns what could be a mundane vacation into a minisabbatical. "When the aircraft leaves the runway, I give up all the things I did not get done and would have liked to, and all my business thoughts. It took me a long time to be able to do this. Now, mentally I am off for an adventure. There is no communication to the office. We sail. We have a boat phone on the sailboat that was installed by the charter company, but we have never hooked it up."

What happens away from the phones and the schedules? "I come home with focus, energy, vitality, and anecdotes that are great in my business. Not only that, I come home with healthy relationships with my husband and family, and ultimately they are my best and most important fans. If I have learned anything in the past five years of my life, it has been the knowledge that time away from achieving fuels my success. P.S. I sail 6 weeks per year. My life/work design is to extend it to 12 weeks off and still to continue to increase my income."

Pagano also practices short-term versions of the sabbatical, as a kind of quick charge. She will schedule a day with no agenda. She does just whatever the moment holds. For her, that means not getting out of her pajamas, unplugging the phone, watching old movies, or lying in bed reading a novel. But for that one day, nothing goes, except what she decides from hour to hour. "I do it once every few months," she says. "It's great."

Fran Tarkenton, entrepreneur and former pro quarterback, believes it makes good management sense not only to take sabbaticals yourself but also to arrange for your employees to take them. In fact, Tarkenton *insists* that his top executives take off one entire month each year.

Many of my interviewees have learned to let their breaks coincide with the slack time of their work cycle. Malcolm Forbes, Jr., uses a week before Christmas and a week during the doldrums of summer for family-related breaks. Learning to let go is a way of avoiding becoming bored, burning out. If you stay in the same routine, working with the same people in the same spaces, hearing the same responses you've grown accustomed to, your mind becomes stagnant.

Singer and composer Billy Joel doesn't use the word *sabbatical* to describe the way he restores his creative powers. He used a term from agriculture. "There are times when you need to let the field *lie fallow*," he told me. This talented composer and performer is describing what farmers often do: They will let a plot rest, rotating crops through the field, letting some parts lie fallow so that they can replenish themselves. The same thing is true of creativity. There's a time to produce and a time not to. Once you get to know that, you don't have to fear burnout so much.

When Billy Joel finishes a road tour, sometimes it will be months before he tries to write again. During that time, sometimes he will go to sea in his boat, leaving the land far behind; it's just him against the elements. Sometimes he will take his family along and be just regular folks. Sometimes he will stay at home and play with his child. And sometimes he will read—fiction, nonfiction, poetry, even textbooks and encyclopedias.

When Billy Joel is treating his creative powers like fallow ground, he avoids using them so that later on he can use them again. The mind, like a farmer's field, can give only so much. After a time, it becomes exhausted, drained of its power to produce abundant harvests.

This tactic isn't for everyone. Few people have the financial means to work at nothing for weeks or months on end. But even people with limited means can save for and do minisabbaticals.

ॐ

TAKE THE ROAD LESS TRAVELED

The line that is the title of M. Scott Peck's famous book comes from Robert Frost's poem "The Road Not Taken," published in 1916.

> Two roads diverged in a wood, and I—
>
> I took the one less traveled by,
>
> And that has made all the difference.

Occasionally, get off the expressway and take a side road, literally and figuratively. The side road will take you longer to get you where you are going, but you will make discoveries that you'll never make on the expressway.

You may want to take these excursions on evenings, weekends, or holidays. Those are certainly good times to meander. But you may want to take a side trip during the workweek, too. The "road" may take you to the library to read just for fun, or to the golf course, as long as golf is not a part of a regular routine. What you want to do is something out of the ordinary, so to avoid the well-worn grooves of your life.

Try something new: a new way to work, a different radio station, or a different breakfast cereal. Break out of your old mold occasionally, with a new way to dress, a different hobby or vacation place.

The road less traveled can be a reward after a demanding event, a carrot that you reward yourself with. Or it can be a good way to loosen up before the big event.

Bobby Dodd, the legendary football coach at Georgia Tech who won six straight major bowl games, knew the power of this tactic. While other coaches were putting their teams through brutal twice-a-day practices, getting bruised and tired, Bobby Dodd's teams did their drills and practices but then took time to relax, play touch football, and enjoy the bowl sites of New Orleans, Jacksonville, and Miami. Did the idea work? Six straight times.

The long way home may yield some wonderful surprises. S. I. Hayakawa was already a world-recognized scholar, college president, and author prior to his becoming the U.S. senator from California. His book *Language in Thought and Action* sold many thousands of copies and went through numerous editions.

I asked the Senator, then in his 80s, how he wanted to be remembered, to which he gave the following remarkable reply:

> I'd like them to say, "He sure got around." I have lots of interests. I'm interested in politics. I'm interested in semantics. I'm interested in academic life. I was deeply, deeply interested in psychology....I earned credentials in anthropology and jazz history. I've taken up scuba diving. One thing that continues to motivate me is the unknown around the corner, and I think that people condemn themselves to premature death by saying, "I'm a tool-maker," "I'm a dentist," "I'm a professor." When they retire you, you're no longer a tool-maker, a dentist, or a professor, so what else is there to do except die? And if that's the way you look at yourself, then you do condemn yourself to death. So far as I'm concerned, I don't know what I am....I don't know what's going to happen next, but I want to experience a lot of things before I die....The possibilities of this vast, rich, exciting world are infinite. Life is very, very short, so you've got to get around. And so you asked me what you want historians to say of me after I'm dead. I'd like for them to say: "Well, he got around."

❧
CUT YOURSELF SOME SLACK

You don't have to do everything. Just do what's important. So, let some things go. You can't be intense all the time—just when it's necessary. So, be gentle with yourself sometimes.

There's nothing wrong with pushing yourself hard, disciplining yourself to do what needs to be done because it must be done, when you hold yourself to the very highest standards. That builds up stamina and turns you into a pro. But there must be some times when you forgive yourself. You will never become 100 percent time-efficient, nor should you expect to be. After something didn't work out, ask yourself, "Did I do the very best I could?" If you did, accept the outcome. All you can do is all you can do.

Garnett Keith has a big job. As vice chairman of Prudential Insurance Company of America, he is responsible for the company's multi-billion-dollar investments worldwide. Keith says he doesn't always follow the rules that he's found in most time management books. He sometimes will let a meeting run longer than it's supposed to, deliberately. Why? Because Keith believes that one of the main reasons for having a meeting is to bond people together. And that sometimes takes extra time.

As he sees it, a big company is held together by its managers, by its officers, and it's important for them to know one another and trust one another. Keith told me, "I get my work done by delegating to other people. I'm not going to delegate to somebody if I don't trust them, if I don't have confidence in their ability. So if a meeting doesn't end precisely when it should, but emotional bonding is taking place, that's more important for me than quitting on time."

Keith understands that it's more important to be *effective* than efficient. He watches the clock much of the time. In fact, he was 15 minutes early for our breakfast appointment. But he also understands that there are times when staying on schedule is not the best way to be effective. For Garnett Keith, what happens in a meeting is more important than when it starts and when it ends.

Austin McGonigle advises salespeople always to allocate twice the amount of time that they think might be necessary for a key sales call. The customer might want to go into some of the minute details of a proposal. Or he or she might get excited about the proposal and want to call in a key associate to take a look at it, too. If salespeople tightly schedule back-to-back calls, they create a dilemma for themselves. They have to decide whether to cultivate the situation at hand and run late to their next appointment, or rush the situation and be on time for the next one.

By allowing more time than you might need, you will often find yourself with downtime to make use of. But it's better to have to deal with downtime than to rush an important meeting just as it's beginning to unfold. The best time tacticians avoid scheduling appointments so tightly that they have to make those kinds of choices. They allow time for things to go right.

ॐ

BLUR THE BOUNDARIES

One way to achieve balance between the work that you do and the life that you live is to blur the boundaries between them. That's the recommendation of author and consultant Alan Weiss. Weiss says he has unabashedly tried to earn a lot of money because he views money as a means to an end. "About 8 or 10 years ago, I realized that there shouldn't be a rigid line between work and pleasure," he told me. "So I blurred the line deliberately. I work out of my home. At times, at 2:00 in the afternoon, I'm at the pool where I'm watching my kids play sports or I'm reading a book or I'm out with my wife. At times, on a Saturday, or at 10:00 in the evening during a weekday, I might be doing some client work. I do things when the spirit moves me and I do things when they're appropriate. I try to get my priorities in order that way."

A number of other highly successful people achieve the balance by setting aside certain days for the family, or perhaps an extended period of time with them after a long period of work. (This is one of the time tactics mentioned previously.) Not Weiss. He finds this arrangement burdensome and artificial. "What I've found is, if you are engaged in work that is a passion to you, then that passion consumes your personal and professional life and you blur the line. Consequently there's a wonderful balance in your life because you're doing both things all the time. The balance is achieved by realizing that there's this wholeness that you can obtain by recognizing that your personal life reinforces your professional life and your professional life reinforces your personal life. So, I have no qualms about working a half day or taking a day off. I also have no qualms about working a 15-hour day. It really depends on what has to be done and how the spirit moves me."

Weiss's advice is not for everyone or every occupation. Some careers don't lend themselves to this strategy. Some jobs must get done in unpleasant or isolated or dangerous surroundings. One of my clients is Marathon Oil Company. Some of the managers I work with spend extended periods of time on platforms in inhospitable places like the North Sea. No amount of positive thinking can make some of their tasks very pleasant, nor can family or close friends always be close at hand.

But blurring the boundaries is possible more often than most people think. One way is to involve people you care about in what you do for a living. They need not get involved in day-to-day activities, but they can keep up with your field. My daughters have their own careers but they have been deeply involved with several of my projects and have made enormous contributions to them. Many highly successful individuals take their spouses to conferences and meetings. Some conferences have spouse programs and encourage spouses to attend other sessions of the conference. I think this is smart. If people who mean a great deal to you understand what you do for a living, they can share more fully in your successes and failures. They also are more likely to be a good sounding board for your ideas and give you good advice.

ॐ

PLAY SOLITAIRE

Our language has wisely sensed the two sides of being alone. It has created the word "loneliness" to express the pain of being alone. And it has created the word "solitude" to express the glory of being alone.

—PAUL TILLICH[46]

Some of my interviewees have told me that they dislike solitude, certainly long stretches of it. They miss the stimulation of frequent interaction with people. They will choose a space where activity takes place around them. Oscar de la Renta's working desk was in that kind of place. Malcolm Forbes, Jr., told me that he thrives on the stimulation of interaction with others. A CEO told me his idea of misery was two weeks on an isolated beach away from a phone.

But many told me just the opposite. They need time by themselves. Nothing, they said, could quite substitute for solitude.

"I think all great stuff comes out of being alone," says Carolyn Wyeth, the sister of artist Andrew Wyeth, and a fine artist in her own right. "At the time you may feel lonely, but it's doing something wonderful to you."

In Wyeth's case, she recalls that solitude was often imposed upon her when she was a child, when her sisters would run off to the woods and not include her. She learned to amuse herself, to have her own thoughts.[47]

Homer Rice recommends that you take one or two periods a day, 15 to 20 minutes each, in order to relax completely. This can be a time for meditation. But don't expect this recommendation from just anyone. Our society doesn't value solitude very much because our society doesn't put much stock in inner direction. There's often a stigma associated with preferring one's own company to the company of others. Becoming known as a loner can even damage your career.

Some companies grade employees—formally and informally—on how much time they spend with their colleagues. If you don't spend lots of time with them, you run the risk of being looked upon as unfriendly, as not one of the group, not a team player.

So, you may have to find solitary time on the sly—such as before you get to work or in the evenings. You may have to disguise your solitude as long walks or jogging or as swimming. Exercising is socially acceptable, but that's often done in a group setting. You might be able to meditate in some quiet place like the library, a chapel, or a church.

Perhaps playing solitaire has never been much valued by rank-and-file individuals. The Tao Te Ching, written around the fifth century B.C., observed:

Ordinary men hate solitude.

But the Master makes use of it,

Embracing his aloneness, realizing

he is one with the whole universe.

The way you use solitary time should match your values, beliefs, and temperament. Some individuals devote a regular time each day to going over their objectives, visualizing themselves actually attaining them, perhaps reading them aloud. Others read religious books and pray. Others try to avoid conscious thought, slipping into alphalike trance states. Some meditate, using crystals. Some use New Age or Far Eastern approaches, or yoga. For others, solitary time is nothing more exotic than looking at the sunset, the sunrise, the mountains, the sea, or a flower. Find out what works for you.

Whatever form it takes, time devoted to solitariness can have an enormous payoff. Achievers talk about an inner strength they find. They feel more confident about their choices, more self-reliant. They talk about how it helps them put competing demands into perspective. They discover a sense of balance, a centeredness.

Successful living and successful time management involve getting along with others and getting along with yourself. "In order to live well," M. Scott Peck says, "we have to negotiate a kind of tightrope between two extremes, to have x amount of togetherness and x amount of separateness."[48]

❧
ENLIST IN PEACETIME PATRIOTISM

Joe Posner is an active life insurance man who has achieved wealth and recognition in his profession. He is a member of the Million Dollar Roundtable and has presented to that prestigious organization. He could retire but has chosen not to. Several years ago, Posner became concerned about what was happening to the children who were growing up in the slums of his hometown of Rochester, New York. Posner is an avid reader of history and is convinced that high civilizations often fail because the people at the top do not pay enough attention to people at the bottom, especially the children of people at the bottom. So Posner helped form a group of successful private enterprise-oriented citizens to develop and perfect early childhood educational preschooler programs to prepare inner city children to complete their education cycles and help break the poverty cycle.

Posner calls what he's doing *peacetime patriotism.* Isn't that a great concept? Posner believes that citizens should work just as hard in peacetime to hold the country together as they do against an outside foe. He wants to enlist people who believe like he does to expand inner city early childhood preschooler education all over the nation.

You may not work with children. You may find some other equally worthy cause that needs doing. It may be for your church or a hospital board, as Bill Marriott, Jr., does, or it may be for a civic club or your alumni association. Many time tacticians have told me they find balance and fulfillment doing pro bono work after quitting time.

For over a decade now, many Americans have had little time for causes and philanthropies. So many have been so busy with their own careers that some observers have called this the "me generation." Individual achievement has been "in." Causes have been "out."

Unfortunately, all the requirements of a good society do not get met if everybody limits themselves to their own narrowly defined careers. In a good society, individuals care about the *common good.*

There are powerful rewards for balancing personal interests with the needs of the common good. One of the most wonderful is the sheer joy that can come from giving. Indeed, there is a happiness in giving that exceeds that of receiving. Another reward is the better place that you help create.

FIND SOMETHING YOU LOVE TO DO AND DO IT

A theme that was expressed repeatedly when I was interviewing for *The Achievement Factors* is to find something you love and do it. The high achievers always seemed to say that they loved what they did. The late Malcolm Forbes, Sr., told me this is the *foremost quality* for career success.

If you find something that you love to do, doing it can transform what otherwise might be a duty into a joy, what might be dreary into something enchanting. Larry King told me that sometimes he will be tired and perhaps yawning before the show, but, he said, "At nine o'clock, energy occurs when the light goes on. It's unexplainable to me. I think if I can give you some tips, I love what I am doing. I don't *like* it. I *love* it."

TIME TACTICS VERSUS TIME STRATEGIES

Tactics asks the question, "How can I save time?" *Strategy* asks, "What do I save time for?" This book is filled with time tactics—the way very successful people answer the question, "How can I save time?"

The strategic use of time—the What for?—involves a much larger issue. Strategy has to do with being successful—but successful at what? With your career. If somebody else pays your salary, being strategic generally means convincing them that you are spending your time in a way that benefits them. If there's a dispute over how you should use your time, either convince the people who can reward or punish you that your idea about using time is correct, or look for another job.

If you are in business for yourself—as more and more people are—it's absolutely critical to ask continually: What for? Answer that question in terms of your priorities. Establish your priorities by asking the questions that were mentioned in Chapter 2. You may want to go back and look at them again now. Those questions tell you which items should get done first, which items you can let slide, and which items shouldn't even make the list.

Johnnetta Cole sets aside a block of time each week when any student at her college can come to see her. She also teaches one course per year. She's a teaching college president. Why? "Because I need regular reminders to tell me why I'm here," Cole told me.

But you need to ask the "What for?" question about more than career. Career is one part, albeit a significant part, of the larger life we live. Granted, some people become so wrapped up in their jobs that the career is all that they have. When they retire or are fired, they have little else: no identity; no activities that they enjoy doing; few friends, for they often discover that most of their friends have fallen away after they left the job. Their friendships were business friendships. When the business stopped, so did the friendships.

The "What for?" question should be asked about the life you live, not just the work that you do. It is truly a comprehensive question, and gets at the question of wholeness.

Where do you turn to answer the big "What for?" To God? To philosophical and ethical systems? To religious leaders? To the inner heart? To life itself? Only you can answer that question.

In 1930 Albert Einstein, the German-born physicist, participated in a radio interview. He was asked if he had a message to impart to the world and he replied, *"Selbstswerk."* He did not have an English translation for *selbstswerk*, which means essentially, "Final in themselves." Later at a family desk in his library, he wrote the complete quotation (in German): "Never forget that the fruits of our work are not final in themselves. Production is meant to make our lives easier, to give our lives a touch of beauty and refinement, but we should not allow ourselves to be degraded into mere slaves of production."[49]

I personally do not want to be a slave of production. My own "What for?" question involves attaining peace of mind—doing anything and everything that can help achieve it. That may not be your "What for?" But if you want to achieve balance, you will need to know what it is.

Ralph Waldo Emerson wrote a wonderful piece about success that I like very much. It defines success in terms of big attitudes and little acts: "To laugh often and much; to win the respect of intelligent people and affection of children; to earn the appreciation of honest critics and endure the betrayal of false friends; to appreciate beauty, to find the best in others; to leave the world a bit better, whether by a healthy child, a garden patch, or a redeemed social condition; to know even one life has breathed easier because you have lived. This is to have succeeded."

Once you know what your "What for?" question is, how do you achieve it? You achieve it a day at a time, a task at a time. When I was a graduate student, I used to listen to Earl Nightingale on a New Orleans radio station. I liked his program so much that I asked his sponsor to send me the scripts of his program. Recently I found one of those old Earl Nightingale scripts in my files. I'd like to end this book with his words:

> Here's a formula for success that will work every time, for any man or woman on earth: A lifetime consists of years, months, weeks, and days. The basic unit of a lifetime is a single day. And a single day is made up of certain acts which each of us must perform in the arena in which each of us finds himself. We need only perform successfully each act of a single day to have that day be successful. Repeat this each day for a week and you have a successful week, and so on. If you will only do each day the things you know you should do each day...and do them as successfully as you possibly can...you can rest assured that you will be successful all the years of your life....
>
> You don't have to run around in circles trying to do a great many things. It isn't the number of acts you perform...but rather the efficiency with which you perform them that counts. Don't try to do tomorrow's work today...or next week's. Just do today's work as best you can, and leave tomorrow's work for tomorrow. That's really all there is to it.
>
> Your job then is to play out the game you have been given to the best of your ability. Success is nothing more, or less, than this....The happiest and most contented people are those who each day do their acts...all of them...as best they can.

Notes

1. Alexandra Biesada, "Best-Practice Companies: Merck Sharp & Dohme," *Financial World*, September 17, 1991, pp. 41, 42.

2. Jimmy Calano and Jeff Salzman, *CareerTracking: Twenty-Six Success Shortcuts to the Top*. New York: Simon and Schuster, 1988, pp. 63–65.

3. Mark H. McCormack, *What They Don't Teach You at Harvard Business School*. New York: Bantam Books, 1984, pp. 210–212.

4. Ken Cooper, *Always Bear Left, and Other Ways to Get Things Done Faster and Easier*. New York: Dell, 1982.

5. Quoted in Horace Freeland Judson, *The Eighth Day of Creation: Makers of the Revolution in Biology*. New York: Simon and Schuster, 1979, p. 20.

6. *Success,* November 1991, p. 14.

7. Alvin Moscow, *The Rockefeller Inheritance*. New York: Doubleday, 1977, p. 73.

8. Betty Edwards, *Drawing on the Right Side of the Brain: A Course in Enhancing Creativity and Artistic Confidence*. Los Angeles: J. P. Tarcher, 1979, p. 57.

9. Gamaliel Bradford, *The Quick and the Dead*. Dallas: Taylor Publishing, 1969, p. 117.

10. P. M. Zall, "Abe Lincoln Laughing," in Gabor S. Boritt, *The Historian's Lincoln: Pseudohistory, Psychohistory, and History*. Urbana: University of Illinois Press, p. 13.

11. Albert Bigelow Paine, *Mark Twain*. New York: Harper and Brothers, 1912, p. 741.

12. Susan Lark, "Low Energy Blues," *The Energy Times,* vol. 2, no. (2), pp. 16, 19 [no date].

13. Don Belt, "Sweden in Search of a New Model," *National Geographic*, vol. 184, no. (2), 16, August 1993.

14. Martin E. P. Seligman, *Learned Optimism*. New York: Knopf, 1991, pp. 276–277.
15. John Gunter, *Roosevelt in Retrospect*. New York: Harper and Brothers, 1950, pp. 32, 33.
16. Russell Baker, "My Best Cellar," *Lear's*, August 1990, pp. 66–68.
17. Ibid.
18. C. Northcote Parkinson, *Parkinson's Law and Other Studies in Administration*. Boston: Houghton Mifflin, 1957, p. 2.
19. B. Eugene Griessman, *The Achievement Factors: Candid Interviews with Some of the Most Successful People of Our Time*. New York: Dodd, Mead, 1987. Now published in paperback by Pfeiffer (San Jose, CA).
20. Clara Clemens, *My Father, Mark Twain*. New York: Harper, 1931. J. P. Frosthoffer, *Horizon*. Elmira, NY, June 1988, pp. 17–18.
21. Helen Gurley Brown, *Having It All*. New York: Pocket Books, 1983, p. 30.
22. *Faust: Vorspiel auf dem Theater* (1806), as translated by John Anster, *Faust: A Dramatic Mystery, Prelude of the Theater* (1835) in Burton Stevenson (ed.), *The Home Book of Quotations*. New York: Dodd, Mead, 1956, p. 2298g.
23. "Neil Simon's Pinball Rules for Playwriting,"*The New York Times,* March 22, 1992, p. H5.
24. Herbert A. Simon, *Models of My Life*. New York: Basic Books, 1991.
25. John Russell's review of Norris Houghton, *Entrances and Exits: A Life In and Out of the Theatre*. (New York: Limelight Editions) in *The New York Times* Book Review Section, August 18, 1991, p. 2.
26. Robert Tyer Jones, Jr., *Golf Is My Game*. Garden City, NY: Doubleday, 1960, p. 68.
27. Allen N. Schoonmaker, *A Students' Survival Manual, Or How to Get an Education Despite It All*. New York: Harper & Row, 1971, pp. 283, 284, 288.
28. Francis Bacon, *Essays: Of Studies,* in Burton Stevenson (ed.), *The Home Book of Quotations*. New York: Dodd, Mead, 1956, p. 1672:7.
29. Jimmy Calano and Jeff Salzman, op. cit., p. 66.
30. Ralph Waldo Emerson, "Self-Reliance," in N. Saxe Commins and Robert N. Linscott (eds.), *The World's Great Thinkers: The Social Philosophers*. New York: Random House, 1947, p. 390.

31. Kenneth Blanchard, William Oncken, Jr., and Hal Burrows, *The One Minute Manager Meets the Monkey.* New York: William Morrow, 1989.

32. Bill Oncken and Donald Wass, "Managing Management Time: Who's Got The Monkey?" *Harvard Business Review,* November/December 1974.

33. Edmund B. Lambeth, "Gene Roberts," *The Quill,* June 1991, p. 22.

34. See Robert B. Miller, Stephen E. Heiman, and Tad Tuleja, *Strategic Selling: The Unique Sales System Proven Successful by America's Best Companies.* New York: William Morrow, 1985.

35. Peter G. Sassone, "Survey Finds Low Office Productivity Linked to Staffing," *National Productivity Review,* Spring 1992, pp. 147–158.

36. Dale Carnegie, *How to Win Friends and Influence People.* New York: Simon and Schuster, 1936, p. 39.

37. In Notes for a Law Lecture, July 1, 1850, from Bruce Bohle, cited in Burton Stevenson (ed.), *The Home Book of American Quotations,* New York: Dodd, Mead, 1967, p. 226.

38. Scott Winokur, "Scientists Claim They Can Predict Doomed Marriages," *The Atlanta Constitution,* August 29, 1989, pp. B1–B2.

39. Kareem Abdul-Jabbar with Mignon McCarthy, *Kareem.* New York: Random House, 1990, p. 91.

40. Arthur Bloch, *Murphy's Law and Other Reasons Why Things Go Wrong.* Los Angeles: Price/Stern/Sloan, 1979, pp. 4–5.

41. James S. Hirsch, "Flood of Information Swamps Managers, But Some Are Finding Ways to Bail Out, *The Wall Street Journal,* August 12, 1991, p. B1.

42. Don Peppers and Martha Rogers, *The One to One Future: Building Relationships One Customer at a Time.* New York: Doubleday, 1993, pp. 385, 386.

43. Alexis de Tocqueville, *Democracy in America,* vol. 2. New York: Vintage Books, 1945 (1835), pp. 144, 145.

44. Ralph Waldo Emerson, "Self-Reliance," in Saxe Commins and Robert N. Linscott (eds.), *The World's Great Thinkers, volume: Man and Man: The Social Philosophers.* New York: Random House, 1947, p. 392.

45. Alan Loy McGinnis, *The Power of Optimism.* San Francisco: Harper & Row, 1990.

46. Quoted in Bernard Asbell, *What They Know About You.* New York: Random House, 1991, p. 91.

47. Quoted in Helen Gurley Brown, *Having It All.* New York: Pocket Books, 1982, p. 21.

48. "Interview with M. Scott Peck," *Playboy,* March 1991, p. 51.

49. From the autograph catalog of Kenneth W. Rendell Gallery #236, 1993, p. 12.

Index

227

About the Author

B. Eugene Griessman, Ph.D., is a famed speaker, author, media personality, and consultant. He is a frequent guest on television and radio shows and his award-winning productions have aired on WCNN and TBS. Griessman has taught at the College of William and Mary, North Carolina State University, Georgia Tech, and the University of Islamabad, where he was a Fulbright Professor. Winner of the Benjamin Franklin award for books on business and career, Dr. Griessman is author of seven books, plus articles for leading newspapers and magazines. He has written a one-man play on Abraham Lincoln and the book *The Words Lincoln Lived By*. As Lincoln, he has performed at historic Ford's Theatre and at numerous conventions, corporate meetings, schools, and universities.

To schedule Dr. Gene Griessman for a workshop, keynote, or Lincoln portrayal, phone 800-749-GOAL (4625), fax 310-230-9851, email abe@mindspring.com, or visit his website at www.presidentlincoln.com